OUT ~~THE~~
NIGHT

A story of tragedy and hope from a survivor of
the 1959 Montana-Yellowstone earthquake

Irene Bennett Dunn

PLAUDIT PRESS

COPYRIGHT © 1998 by Irene Bennett Dunn

Cover photograph courtesy U.S. Forest Service

Cover and book design by Jackie Oldfield

Published by Plaudit Press, an imprint of
Keokee Co. Publishing, Inc.
P.O. Box 722
Sandpoint, ID 83864
Phone 208/263-3573

ISBN 1-879628-16-3

Printed in the United States of America
First printing

Publisher's Cataloging-in-Publication Data
Dunn, Irene Bennett
    Out of the night : a story of tragedy and hope from a sur-
    vivor of the 1959 Montana-Yellowstone earthquake/ by
    Irene Bennett Dunn

    1. Dunn, Irene Bennett. 2. Earthquakes - Montana -
    Personal narratives.

920 - dc21

Dedication

This book is dedicated to the memory of my family lost in the 1959 Montana-Yellowstone earthquake, and to my surviving son, Phil.

Acknowledgments

My indebtedness includes my son Phil and husband, Jack, who brought happiness into my life a second time. Their patience has been outstanding while I've worked on this book. Phil gave me strong support, input and approval and Jack became a good sounding board, helpful critique and my first editor.

We're gratefully indebted to Dr. Losee and staff at Madison Valley Hospital in Ennis, Montana for wonderful caring treatment, for spiritual guidance from Pastor Jack Hawthorne of the Nazarene Church in Coeur d' Alene, Idaho and the kind support and help from both Purley's (Pud) family and my family at this time. We also thank our many Hope friends and neighbors of Dalton Gardens who gave us support and help in many ways.

I thank my longtime friend, Harriet Walker, for encouraging me to write my memoirs. She invited me to attend an Idaho State Writer's League Conference and we later joined the Sandpoint chapter. I include too, all my Idaho Writer friends who helped me with this story. Their tolerance at hearing rewritten chapters kept me stimulated.

My thanks to Chris Bessler, Billie Jean Plaster and Jackie Oldfield of Keokee Co. Publishing for their kindness and wonderful help in getting this book published.

Table of Contents

The Forest Service erected this plaque in 1960 near the landslide area as a memorial for the 28 victims. The plaque reads the following:

This monolith is part of the huge slide caused by the earthquake of August 17, 1959. It is dedicated to the memory of the men, women and children whose lives were lost as a result of the earthquake.

In Memoriam

Sidney D. A. Ballard
Margaret Ballard
Christopher Thomas Ballard
Purley R. Bennett
Tom O. Bennett
Carole Bennett
Susan Bennett
Bernie L. Boynton
Inez Denda Boynton
Merle M Edgerton, M.D.
Edna Mae Edgerton
Margaret Duffey Holmes
Myrtle L. Painter
Roger C. Provost

Elizabeth Findlay Provost
Richard Provost
David Provost
Thomas Mark Stowe
Marilyn Whitmore Stowe
Edgar H. Stryker
Ethel M. Stryker
Robert James Williams
Edith Coy Williams
Steven Russell Williams
Michael James Williams
Christy Lyn Williams
Harmon Woods
Edna Maude Woods

Introduction

The Montana-Yellowstone earthquake of major magnitude in August of 1959 convulsed an area of 600,000 square miles in northwestern America. The Richter magnitude scale registered 7.5 compared to San Francisco's 8.25 in 1906. Eighty million tons of a 7,600 foot mountain toppled into the Madison River. A 3,000 ton boulder and another only slightly smaller were hurled across the river and up a mountain on the other side to come to rest almost a mile away. The massive slide dammed the river and formed a new body of water, Earthquake Lake. The shock which caused the slide tilted seven-mile-long Hebgen Lake. Cottages on one side were inundated and cottages on the other side left high and dry. The tremor was felt in nine Western states and parts of Canada. Seven weeks after the first major shock, which came at 11:37 on the night of August 17, 1959, the region was still experiencing a minimum of 55 shocks a day.

In memory of those who lost their lives, the Forest Service placed a bronze plaque on a large dolomite rock at the Interpretive Center. Among the names of the victims listed are Purley R. Bennett, Carole I. Bennett, Tom O. Bennett, and Susan E. Bennett.

*Above: The massive landslide that devastated Rock Creek Campground.
Below: The Bennett's car after being tossed out from under the landslide.
Photos courtesy of the U.S. Forest Service*

Chapter 1

Tragedy

"What's happening?" my husband Pud shouted as we awakened to an incredible rumbling sound. Struggling to gain a foothold, he grasped a small tree while strong winds pulled at his body. Rushing water overtook us and I remember being swept away by it. My next awareness was finding myself on a wet, sandy, river bank with a tree lying across my back. I sensed the shaking earth while the moon shone brightly over the mountain. The vibration and the beating of my heart seemed in steady rhythm. Lying on the trembling ground my heart throbbed, my mind bursting with anxious thoughts for my husband and children. I began to dig myself out from under the tree. Cold, wet, and naked; my clothes had been stripped from me by wind and water. I dug ... rested ... dug ... and rested ... dug more ... and rested ... till at last I could pull myself free. Survival is one's strongest desire.

Hoping to locate loved ones, my naked body shaking with the earth, I called, "Pud, where is everyone?" No answer – just dead silence. Where's my baby Susan? She's only five and needs me to comfort her. "Susan, it's Mama where are you? Tom, I'm here." He's only eleven and probably very frightened. Where are my teenagers? "Carole, do you hear me? Phil, are you here? Please someone answer me, it's Mom!"

More silence! I prayed to God, asking for his help. Looking at the moon I recited the 121st Psalm learned as a teenager. "I will lift up mine eyes unto the hills, from whence cometh my help." The hills appeared as if a line were drawn on them with the earth shaking below; dirt rolled out of the fault line. I pulled branches over my naked body for protection from the cold; my flesh rippled with goose-bumps. I continued to pray. Someone once said, "If man has enough faith he can find his way in the dark – with faith as his lamp." I sensed a heavenly presence around me and knew He would see me to safety. "The Lord is thy keeper," the Psalm said.

I remained there praying all night, my heart and the earth keeping an anxious beating rhythm as I endured continuous after-shocks. I called and called my family but heard no answers.

When daylight dawned and I could see around me, I crawled, being unable to stand, down towards the river bed. I repeatedly called. "Pud, I'm here. Kids, it's Mom, where are you?" AT LAST, I heard an answer.

"Mom?"

What a wonderful sound! Phil, my sixteen year old, had seen our car and was crawling towards it when he heard the sound of my voice.

"Yes, Phil, it's me Mom," I answered.

Until this time the only thing I'd found relating to family was Phil's belt which I clutched in my hand.

By the sound of our voices we reached each other down in the empty river bed. Seeing him made my heart almost cease beating. His leg looked like a letter S dragging behind him as he pulled himself towards me with blood flowing from cuts behind his ear and the top of his head. Both our bodies were scraped, bloody, and bruised. However, the importance of the moment was we'd found each other. We continued to call family members but no answer came.

Hearing planes overhead, we tried to signal but to no avail. After a seeming eternity we began to hear voices. We called, "Help! We're over here!" Our prayers were answered, rescuers had arrived! A kind lady brought blankets. Wonderful not only for warmth but the embarrassment of being nude.

Anxiety for other members of the family was uppermost in our minds. "Please find the rest of our family. My husband and three more children are here somewhere." Giving their descriptions was important for the search to begin.

Searchers found my husband's body before we left the river. I remember the lady who brought blankets gave me the sorrowful news. Tears engulfed me; my heart throbbed, knowing

I'd lost Pud and our happy life together had ended. Giving me a handkerchief, she said, "Here, dear, use this and go ahead and cry." She stayed with me through my first overpowering grief.

Rescuers carried us across the river bed to waiting vehicles where Dr. Ronald Losee administered first aid. Phil's injuries were most serious. They put us in a pick-up, the first vehicle available, and Dr. Losee rushed us to the Madison Valley Hospital in Ennis, Montana with us being unaware of what happened to the rest of the family.

After arrival at the hospital they settled us in rooms following some clean-up and made us comfortable as possible. Dr. Losee rendered heartwarming care and put Phil in traction for both the broken leg and collar bone. Thus began the healing of our wounds.

Chapter 2

Pud

Enveloped with grief, my whole life with Pud swept rapidly before my eyes.

I first met Purley (Pud) Bennett at my grandparent's home in Nebraska. He came from Hope, Idaho, with his father and brother to visit relatives. My uncle had moved to Hope the year before and sent apples, canned huckleberries, cherries, and venison to our families. As typical teenage girls, my cousin and I had an interest in boys and enjoyed meeting these young men.

In 1936, when my family also moved to Hope, we again met the Bennetts and became friends. I dated Pud off and on for almost five years. We enjoyed each others' company, attending movies and dances and often riding the school bus to basketball games. We corresponded during the summer when he worked for the Forest Service in Blister Rust camps, ridding our forests of currant bushes which caused a fungus disease on white pine trees. We became close friends. One time while getting ready to attend a dance with him, my young sister teased, "You really like Pud don't you? Are you in love?"

I told her and my Mother, "I think of him as a dear brother. His sister, Beryl Ann and I are best friends and in their home they treat me as family."

The Bennett family moved from Hope to Ellensburg, Washington, and I dated others including Jack Dunn during my senior year of high school.

The year after graduation I attended National Youth Administration (NYA) School in Coeur d'Alene, Idaho. During my year at this dormitory I received an excellent education in all aspects of homemaking and sewing. The Bennett's moved back to Hope and Pud's sister attended NYA School too. Soon, Pud and I began dating again with more of an interest than friendship. When he came to see me or I received a letter, my heart would thump and I wondered if I'd fallen in love.

In the fall when Pud and his folks planned a trip to Nebraska to visit his grandmother he said, "I want to take you with me." Realizing this as a proposal, we talked briefly of marriage. He said, "I'll talk with my parents."

A bit unsure about his plan I said, "Well, you can ask them."

He came back to me with the decision, "They aren't ready for us to marry yet. They like you but think we should wait awhile."

Pud and his parents left; we corresponded

and exchanged Christmas gifts. I did housework in people's homes during which time I dated a friend. Pud dated in Nebraska. This caused a bit of jealousy since we felt meant for each other.

When he returned in the spring we found our love had grown stronger. In the summer we married in a double wedding with his sister, Beryl Ann, and her fiance, Leroy Decker. She and I shopped together for dresses. In making arrangements for our informal wedding, I insisted, "I want a Pastor of a Christian Church to perform our marriage. I don't want a Justice of the Peace." The others agreed and we had a proper ceremony in the Christian parsonage in Coeur d'Alene, Idaho. The pastor gave us good advice saying, "Never go to bed without solving your differences." On our wedding night we had a nice room at the Desert Hotel in Coeur d'Alene.

We settled in a small two room house on the Blue Star Dairy farm out of Coeur d'Alene where Pud and his Dad, John Bennett, were in partnership. We lived there eleven years enlarging our house as three children made us a family. Along with being a mother and homemaker, I helped in the milk house bottling "Natural Milk-Naturally Good" for house-to-house delivery in the city of Coeur d'Alene. We had busy years and worked hard to keep things going with our young family.

When anticipating the arrival of our first baby Pud asked, "Will you be too busy to have time for me?"

"Of course not." I answered."You're very important to both the baby and me. I'll have love for you both." Our little girl, Carole Irene, arrived and our love grew stronger as she matured.

When our second child, Philip Richard arrived, Pud said, "I love you so much because you give me such nice babies." Five years later our second son, Tom Orville came and love continued to grow along with our family. We had a good relationship and enjoyed our offspring.

A good worker and provider, a kind and honest person with a great sense of humor describes Pud well. Being a good Christian man he never did wrong intentionally. I always felt fortunate to have someone love me and respect my thoughts as he did.

After Pud's Dad couldn't work the dairy anymore and Pud and I were unable to handle it alone, the cattle were sold and later the farm. Pud went to work for Atlas Building Center in Coeur d'Alene, delivering lumber. We moved to Dalton Gardens close to school, which made it more convenient for our daughter

Pud in the summer of 1956.

who'd had polio. There our second daughter, Susan Elaine, the fourth and last child was born.

A good father to his children Pud enjoyed all of their activities at school and church and participated busily in Boy Scouting with his boys. When Phil would be working on merit badges, his Dad always helped. Phil put in long hours to earn his God and Country award with help both from home and our Pastor while striving towards becoming an Eagle Scout. This he attained along with earning a bronze feather.

I remember Phil studying astronomy and Pud saying, "Come on, Phil, let's go gaze at the stars." Pud had great interest in the universe and I often think how excited he would have been over the NASA program. I thought of him when the astronauts began their exploration of space and when man walked on the moon.

I became a Den Mother when Tom joined Cub Scouts. He and his Dad worked together on many projects.

Our family had many pleasant fishing, camping, and picnic outings enjoying togetherness. I'll never forget the picnic when the fellows hurried to fish. They got up from the table not realizing the slope of the ground or their all being on one side. Ker-Pow! Over it went, Carole and I on the ground with fried chicken, potato salad, and the Kool-Aid jug flying through the air. No injuries developed and we had a good laugh. This delayed the fishing a wee bit but gave us an enjoyable memory.

Now after the experiences at the earthquake

site, I felt devastated as I wept, thinking of Pud being gone and not having more happy times together or his love and care ever again. I made a promise to God and myself I'd do my best to raise our children as he would have wanted. The immediate matter now was finding them.

1952 family picture, clockwise from left:
Pud, Irene, Phil, Carole and Tom.

Chapter 3

On Our Way

During the days of hospitalization I thought back to August 15, when our family prepared to leave on this long planned vacation. My husband had two weeks off and there had been much discussion of where we should travel. Would it be to Canada or Yellowstone Park? We seemed to lean toward Yellowstone as the younger children would enjoy it. We'd been there in 1951 when Tom, now eleven, was only two. Susan, almost six would enjoy the animals. We wanted a nice trip together as a family before Carole, seventeen and Phil, sixteen, would be venturing out into the world on their own.

Leaving our home in care of the Bennett grandparents, we packed and headed out. We spent the first night with my Mother and sister's family in the little town of Hope, Idaho. The cousins had a great time playing. When ready to leave the next morning Tom and his cousin Ruthann, insisted on one more trip to the lake.

Finally all assembled, we proceeded with destination still being a question. The relatives knew our uncertainty.

A few miles down the road we had to make a decision. Pud asked, "Where to, will it be Yellowstone Park or Canada?"

We held a discussion with Susan shouting, "Animals, Animals, I want to see the bears!"

Tom said, "I'd like to see the animals in Yellowstone Park too."

The teenagers agreed since they felt the younger ones would like Yellowstone.

"Ok, if everyone is agreeable, Yellowstone Park it will be."

We drove into Montana staying overnight in a roadside park. Being prepared to camp and cook out, we fixed hash-brown potatoes and eggs for breakfast the next morning and ventured forth. The kids chattered and enjoyed traveling. Susan, who would start first grade in September, kept taking off her thongs and slipping into her school shoes. "It'll be fun to be in first grade." she said. "Do my new shoes look nice?"

When arriving in the Virginia City, Montana area in the afternoon, Phil asked, "What are all those piles of stuff?"

His Dad answered, "Those are old mine tailings. It's what's left after they have taken the minerals out of the rocks they mined here."

"Boy, they must have mined a lot from the looks of the piles."

We stopped at the house called Rustler's Roost where rustlers had hid out from vigilantes. This created interest to learn more about the robbers. Upon entering the restored city we drove down the street and Phil spotted the museum. "Let's go there and find out about the robbers."

"Ok" said Dad, "We'll do that and then take in the rest of the village."

We wandered through the museum learning more about the area and the robbers including the story of Clubfoot George. Also about Boot Hill where many criminals caught by the vigilantes had been buried.

After seeing many things there, we toured the restored shops. We visited the old Pharmacy filled with many bottles of old fashioned medicines. Next we wandered through the Hotel, dress shops, and the old Post Office. Before we entered the Bale of Hay Saloon, Tom spotted an old stagecoach coming down the street. "Oh, look! Daddy can we take a ride in the stagecoach?"

"Yes," he said, "If Phil will hold Susan carefully. Mama and I'll wait here by the saloon where they'll let you off."

When the children came back from their ride excited about Boot Hill, Phil asked, "Can't we all go up and look around? Maybe we can find the grave of Clubfoot George we read about in the museum."

After visiting the Old Saloon and listening to many old time juke boxes playing, we drove up Boot Hill and found Clubfoot George's grave. This fascinated Phil. Touring other interesting buildings and taking lots of pictures we had a fun day together.

We drove through Madison Valley into Ennis, Montana and toward West Yellowstone. Making camp late along the Madison River we had an evening snack. Other campers close by passed our camp going for water at the river. With the moon and bright stars, we spread our tent on the ground with our sleeping bags on top to enjoy the beauty around us. We all liked sleeping under the stars, and everyone settled for the night.

At 11:37 p.m. August 17, 1959 our world changed.

This may have been the last picture of the Bennett children together, taken spring of 1959.

Chapter 4

Tender Care

Phil's and my rescue and care of our physical beings seemed important now. We felt extreme sadness for his father's death but still held anxiety for the children. Where were they? We prayed they'd be found alive. In the little hospital at Ennis, Montana, Dr. Losee and his staff thoroughly examined, x-rayed, and cared for us tenderly.

Doc spent our first night at the hospital by Phil's bedside. I marveled at his professional devotion to his patients. He had wrapped Phil's head and placed him in traction for both the broken collar bone and his mangled leg. Phil experienced the utmost discomfort and asked Doc, "Couldn't I have this arm taken out of traction?"

After deep thought he said, "Boy, you have enough to bear. Your collar bone may heal a bit overlapped but will be minor." Thus he took traction off the shoulder.

My injuries were less serious than Phil's. My

only break was a bone in my lower leg and not my pelvis as first suspected. The deep, badly torn laceration in my thigh took extended time healing. I did have chest and neck muscle damage and my ears required irrigating to rid them of debris. Our bodies were beaten and bruised from head to toe.

Phil's leg was broken in several places and would require surgery. To our advantage Doctor Losee had recently returned from having studied advanced orthopedic surgery in Montreal, Canada. However, our biggest worry at the moment continued to be the head and ear wound as spinal fluid drained from behind his ear. Dr. Losee told me, "If the draining doesn't stop by Wednesday morning I have a specialist alerted in Great Falls and we'll do surgery." The next day tension overpowered me. My mind wrought with worry of losing my son I prayed, "Lord, spare this child."

Dr. Losee came to my room Wednesday morning, "Irene, we won't need to call the specialist. The draining has stopped."

I responded with tears. "Oh! I'm so thankful. The Lord is answering my prayers."

After being hospitalized for several days and getting my thoughts together, I asked a nurse, "What really happened?"

She explained, "An earthquake registering the magnitude of 7.5 on the Richter Scale caused Hebgen Dam on the Madison River here in eastern Montana to overflow and the mountain to fall. Being swept away by the water, rocks, and debris from behind the dam caused your bodies to be totally bruised and beaten. Irene, you and Phil do not have one spot on your bodies that is not scraped, bruised, torn, or broken in some way."

Again I sensed a caring God and said, "Why do you think He saved us? Perhaps someday we'll know."

The hospital personnel provided splendid care. The whole town and community around Ennis showed exceptional friendship and compassion – a cherished memory. Many kind visitors we didn't know came, including pastors who prayed with us. I remember the Catholic priest who came many times. He knew of my Protestant faith but asked, "Would you like me to pray with you?"

I remember answering, "Yes, I'd appreciate your prayers for we all pray to the same God."

Letters and donations came from our home town. I shed many tears while reading wonderful expressions of sympathy and wishes for our recovery. We heard from places all over the United States and the world with words of kindness. We heard from Dr. Losee's Mother in Scotland and friends of mine in France and New Zealand. We valued this incredible kindness.

Days passed involving cleanup of our bodies; our hair was matted and filled with pine needles. We had dried blood to be soaked off, and our bodies cleaned from the force of brush, rocks, wind and water. This care plus more x-rays and interviews by reporters became strenuous. I continued to give information which might help others find family members while awaiting news of our missing loved ones.

After repeating the same story many times Dr. Losee stopped my being questioned; his thoughtfulness helped because I had become emotionally exhausted. Devastated with grief over the loss of Pud and anxiety about Phil, plus wondering ... were my other children alive or badly wounded? Were they calling for me somewhere? I prayed they would be found alive. In my shocked state I was unaware of time. The search for bodies continued.

Chapter 5

Carole

At last we received the message a family member had been found. It was Carole, our teenager. She had not survived. Sadness overpowered me as I thought of never having my daughter to love and share joys with again. I cried for her never getting to finish high school and be loved and have children of her own as I'd done. Her life flashed though my mind.

I thought back to the birth of this child, my first baby. What a miracle! Giving birth was a marvelous experience along with her Daddy's excitement when he saw her. This little one brought pride and joy, and her Daddy named her Carole Irene.

We enjoyed every new little thing she did and loved showing her off to relatives and friends. When she became adventurous in learning to walk, her Daddy came home one day and handed her a little sack. She reached for it and took her first steps alone.

Carole and Phil were "the best of buddies."

When Carole was 15 months old a baby brother, Philip Richard arrived to share the love of her home, making our family doubly proud. Confusion overwhelmed Carole at first but soon she came to love Phil and wanted to help care for him. If he cried and she thought he needed a fresh diaper she'd come bringing one saying, "Mama, baby's pants."

These little ones grew to became the best of buddies. Carole always wanted to mother Phil and look out for his interests. These two, always together, watched over one another. They played house with dolls and wagons. "Let's pretend we're farmers like Mama and Daddy. I'll be the Mama," Carole would say, "and you be the Daddy. You can go get the hay and I'll cook dinner."

The spring before Carole started school another little brother, Tom Orville arrived. The children loved him but were still special to each other.

When Carole's first day of school arrived she bubbled with excitement and put on her red polka-dotted dress with the bunny appliqued on the front. Phil and I took her to meet the school bus. As it drove away he said, "Mama, I don't think she's big enough to go to school." He had a lonely day ahead. Tom, five months old, wasn't much company for him and Carole had always been his playmate.

The day went slow for Phil and he kept asking, "Mama, isn't it time for the bus yet?"

Finally the bus came and Carole arrived home excited saying "Oh, look Mama! We colored this squirrel after we stood and looked at the flag saying something about 'instavegetable.' I'm going to be a teacher when I grow up!" (Instavegetable was her word for indivisible referring to the flag salute.)

Phil wanted her to play, not tell about school. "Hurry and change clothes so we can play."

This little guy spent lonely days for awhile. Daddy fixed the teeter-totter with a tire on one end for Phil to teeter but he missed his buddy. Some days he put on his striped overalls like Dad's and went on the milk route. Other days

Phil would sit and listen to the radio for hours. When they played the song titled, "Life Gets Tegious, Don't It?", he would say, "Mama, don't make any noise, I like this song." I'm sure he felt his life "tegious" without Carole's companionship. After a time he adjusted to playing alone with his tractor and the little man on it. I would hear him say, "Come on George, we've got to move those cattle to another pasture." Sometimes it would be, "George, it's about milking time. Better get the cows in the barn." However, Carole's arrival from school was still the best moment of his day. When she changed to play clothes, these two busy little farm kids enjoyed each other.

Our family did lots of swimming at Coeur d'Alene and Hayden Lake beaches during the summer of 1952. One morning Carole woke saying, "Mama, my throat is sore and I don't feel good." She rested and I watched her. When she didn't seem better we took her to our family doctor. He suspected it might be polio. He gave her gamma globulin shots, but later polio was confirmed.

Because Carole was a shy little girl, the doctor felt it best she be treated at home rather than hospitalized far from her family. The next few months were a trying time for all of us.

We used the Sister Kenny method of treatments consisting of hot packs and massaging many times daily at first, then hot baths and continued massaging three times a day. Her Daddy came from work at noon to help with treatments.

We spent endless hours giving care and therapy under our Doctor Greenwood's careful directions. The only part of her body permanently weakened was her left leg, resulting in minimal shrinkage due to the Sister Kenny treatments.

The illness took a great deal of strength from her little body. She lost lots of weight and calcium from her bones. Drinking two quarts of milk each day, eating liver, plus an abundance of fresh fruits and vegetables became her special necessary diet. Carole disliked liver but ate it because she understood her body's need. She liked green peppers, eating them like apples.

After two weeks the diet amazingly replaced calcium in Carole's bones. Having observed her fluoroscopes a number of times, I was elated at seeing the great improvement this diet had made. Her bones, which had been obscure, now appeared quite normal.

Another time during fluoroscopy I became alarmed. "Doctor, there is a black spot on her chest. What is it?"

At my exclamation of fear Doctor reached under the screen and touched a little pin. "Look here, this is what you are seeing, this little pin on her dress."

"What a relief!" I gasped. Through all this tension we could now laugh a little.

Being a family who believed in God, we prayed together and told Carole, "God truly loves you and His healing strength will help you walk again."

One verse in the Bible most precious to her

was Matthew 17:20 "If ye have faith as a grain of mustard seed, nothing shall be impossible unto you." Carole believed this faithfully and never failed to continue her therapy which she knew would help her walk again. For Christmas we bought her a gold chain with an amulet containing a mustard seed. She treasured this favorite piece of jewelry for it reminded her of God's promise.

During the many months of recuperation, we did all we could to help Carole. Since she was unable to participate in many activities everyone tried to make her happy, including grandparents and brothers. Phil and Tom played many games with her for entertainment.

"Let's play Uncle Wiggley," Tom would say running to get the board game.

Phil would set up the card table where Carole could reach and the fun began. Many enjoyable hours were spent in this manner. By fall Carole attempted walking. She had to have a special shoe and brace fitted to straighten her foot and hold her weight. She wore a brace up to her knee and looked forward to school. I became teacher as well as mother and nurse when school started. With the cooperation of her 5th grade teacher, I helped Carole keep up her studies and she attended school second semester. Phil was always the helpful pal. If I were a bit slow meeting the school bus, this energetic young boy who wanted to run like the wind, would patiently slow down and walk with Carole carrying her books.

At this time the Gideon Professional Business Men's society distributed small Bibles of Psalms, Proverbs, and the New Testament to all 5th graders at their school. Carole loved hers knowing she was receiving help. Reading her little book she'd call to me, "Mama, I found another of my Sunday School memory verses."

Sometimes she would read them to her brothers. Perhaps Phil would say, "Find John 3:16. It's my favorite." Carole would look it up and they would read it together.

"Now let's read the 23rd Psalm." They spent enjoyable times looking up their Sunday School verses. She valued her little book and read in it every day.

The summer of 1954 she needed surgery to straighten her foot. Our family traveled to Boise for this, making it a family vacation. Gramma Coulthard went along to care for the other kids while Pud and I were with Carole at the hospital.

Carole made great improvement after having two surgeries, two broken bones, and several braces along with special shoes to wear. She longed many times to wear penny loafers like other girls her age but seldom complained. This dedicated little girl did her therapy, ate wisely, and rested though she knew the rest of the family had other fun. When Carole became capable of doing more, Phil convinced us to get her a hamster to provide her enjoyment. She loved playing with and caring for her little pet, whom she named "Tillie."

The years progressed and Carole finished

grade school at Dalton Gardens going on to junior high and high school in Coeur d'Alene. She had a slight limp, tired easily but improved. When ready for her senior year she was out of braces and could wear normal girls shoes, finally getting her much longed for penny loafers. This recovery gave her hope of taking part in activities which prior to this time had been impossible. Carole still valued her little Gideon book like a dear friend. It had been a comfort to her during her recuperation years and had drawn our family closer in Christian love. Preparing for our trip Carole had included in her vacation things the little Bible. This most important book went with us but was never found after the quake. Her faith in God was deep and sincere. Tears overwhelmed me and I cried for I'd miss her love, companionship, and seeing her grow to womanhood.

Carole as a junior in high school, 1958.

Chapter 6

Tom

In the hospital, Phil and I had many emotional heartbeats as we shared grief over the loss of two family members. Feeling gratitude for our lives and each other, we prayed Tom and Susan would be found alive.

Continued care of our wounds kept the days busy and full. Phil and I, in two-bed wards had different people with us during this time. When well enough, they wheeled me to his room to see him. As I sat with him, we'd hear drip, drip on the floor from the wound in my thigh. A bit of mopping became necessary after I sat for awhile. I spent more time with him when I could finally walk by myself. During this recuperation period we compared experiences. I learned he too had felt the presence of a Supreme Being. We sensed as the 121st Psalm said, "The Lord shall preserve thy going out and thy coming in from this time forth and even for evermore."

Time being non-existent for us, we received

word another body had been found. This was Tom, my eleven year old son, always such a loving child. With deep grief and tears my mind flashed back over our years since Tom joined the family. The older children loved him and showed enthusiasm whenever he learned something new, whether learning to walk or throw a ball. Being such a busy little guy he always had a project or checked things out by tearing something apart to see how it worked. I remember his Gramma Coulthard giving him a friction wind-up bus for his birthday saying, "Tom, promise me you won't take this apart."

While Carole and Phil attended school, Tom and I spent time together becoming great pals. He also spent time at the grandparent's home when we lived next door to them. They enjoyed having him visit, and it seemed, spoiled him considerably. His fondness for fig-bar cookies they had at their house, often became more than a sufficient amount.

Grampa enjoyed the stories Tom told; he had a fantastic imagination. Grampa found a poem in the paper,"Tommy Tells Tall Tales" describing our four year old to perfection. It related much the same type of stories he told his grandparents.

One day after spending time with the grandparents, Tom came home and said to me, "Mama, I feel so sorry for Grampa and Gramma."

"Why?" I asked.

"I'm sorry they never had any kids."

Of course, I explained to him they'd had children. "Daddy is one of them, Uncle Jack and

Aunt Beryl Ann too. When they were small like you they lived with Grampa and Gramma just like you live with us."

Such confusion for my four year old; it took him some time to straighten out relationship.

Tom greatly enjoyed the companionship of his grandparents and spent all the time he could with them realizing the pleasure they gained from his visits.

He told me, "Mama, what I want to be when I grow up is a Grampa." A real compliment to his Grampa Bennett, a very special person and a super Grampa to each one of his grandchildren.

As Tom became a bit older he would visit an elderly neighbor. Perhaps he felt sorry for her too, being alone with no children.

Tom at Christmas with ice skates and arrows.

At Christmas time one year we had family pictures taken as gifts for relatives. We stressed this would be a surprise and for the children not to tell anyone. Arriving home from the photographers, Tom in his excitement, when seeing the grand-parents said, "I'm not supposed to tell you we had our picture taken for Christmas presents." He had given away the surprise.

However, Tom AND the grandparents kept their secret.

After his Daddy and Grampa sold the dairy, the family moved to Dalton Gardens across from the school. In the fall this happy little boy attended kindergarten from nine to eleven in the mornings. Afternoons he would often visit an elderly couple next door. He always seemed to enjoy older people as friends. Tom and I continued our special times together too, and some afternoons we went with Daddy on a long haul in the lumber truck.

"I will be so glad when I can go to school all day." Tom's anticipation was high. I spent lots of time reading him stories. He would say, "Let's do Nursery Rhymes and read 'Peter Rabbit', Mama." Or perhaps he would come with his favorite little Golden Book, "Dan the Bandage Man". Anxious to read, he'd say "When I go to school I can read by myself!" The other kids read to him too. He and Phil had a room together and often Tom would say, "Let's go to bed so you can read another chapter of "Davy Crockett." Sometimes Daddy and the kids would take turns reading aloud a chapter from favorite books like "Tom Sawyer" or "Huckleberry Finn" before bedtime.

When the new baby's arrival time drew near and I needed to rest afternoons, Tom and I would sometimes nap together or watch the school kids playing in the schoolyard across the street.

When we brought our new baby home, Tom

bubbled with excitement. "I want to take her to kindergarten for show and tell. Can we take her tomorrow, Mama? I want the kids to see our baby."

"Probably not tomorrow, Tom, but one of these days we'll take her." He held great pride for his baby. Susan WAS Tom's show and tell at kindergarten parent-teacher meeting and he enjoyed showing her off. That morning he had gone to my jewelry chest, picked a pair of earrings and brought them to me, "Wear these when you come to the meeting, Mama. I want Susan to wear her little pink dress." He left for school calling, "Be sure and be there at eleven so everyone can see my baby."

When 11 a.m. came we arrived on time dressed as Tom wanted us, not wishing to disappoint him. He helped unwrap Susan. "Come see my baby. Isn't she little? Do you think she's cute?" Never had Tom experienced a prouder moment.

The spring of Tom's seventh birthday, we invited a few friends to help him celebrate. Almost until party time, we weren't sure how many there would be because each day Tom might say, "I invited Marjean to my party. She lives over on the highway next to the station where we get our gas," or "I hope it's ok I asked Kent to my party. He said his Mom would bring him." What started as a small group of close neighborhood friends became quite a party. However we prepared for an unexpected group and all had a great time. Decorations, balloons, ice cream, and cupcakes baked and decorated by Carole made a festive celebration.

The years went by and Tom progressed in school working very hard to learn all the teachers expected of him. When he became a fourth grader he had a teacher who greatly inspired him. At least once a week he prepared necessary items to present a science experiment. He really enjoyed science and said, "None of the kids want to do experiments so I volunteered." He enjoyed giving reports too. We'd recently acquired our new set of encyclopedias and the children enjoyed using them. Tom had everyone helping with his reports. He'd come from school saying, "I'm giving a report on kangaroos Friday. Will someone help me look them up?" Another day it might be, "Tuesday I'm giving a report on the magnetic field." His curious little mind kept us all on the alert.

When Tom had his eleventh birthday we told him he could have a party again. His guest list consisted mostly of girls and it took high persuading to convince him to include more boys from his class. He'd always liked girls since kindergarten. One day he'd come home reporting to the family, "I'm going to marry Phyllis when we grow up."

However, he did include more boys for the party and all had a great time. I am happy for this exceptional birthday as Tom had no more. He never got to grow up and become a "Grampa."

Recently I wrote this poem while reminiscing

my memories of Tom.

Tommy's Pockets

Tommy was a collector,
Of many, many things,
His pockets stuffed with stones and bolts,
And even colored strings.

Some days he collected boards and nails,
And pieces of Mom's old sheet,
Then he'd get Dad's big hammer,
And build a sailing fleet.

Off he'd go to sail them,
In puddles down the lane,
Mother tried to keep him dry,
But found it was in vain.

He had a need to be inventive,
And was curious how things worked,
He treasured pocket goodies,
And his collections he never shirked.

Mom never knew what she would find,
The morning she did the wash,
For among these many objects,
Might be angleworms gone SQUASH!

I cried for this child who would never become a man. With his curious mind, I'd always felt he would further his dreams, for his promises to me had been sincere. I sobbed as I realized the many things I would never see had he been allowed to reach adulthood.

Tears help cover the pain in the heart, but the scar is ever there.

Chapter 7

Susan

We held hope Susan would be found alive; my heart throbbed for her being out there alone.

Healing care filled our days at the hospital and we continued receiving wonderful letters of heartfelt condolences and shed tears while memories flooded our minds.

Several young people of Ennis visited Phil giving him association with his age group. A school teacher from the high school offered to help him with his schooling. He received letters from a Butte High School English class along with souvenirs he treasures to this day.

At last Susan's little body was found. I now sobbed for her missing her first exciting days of school and not having the opportunity to grow up and be a lovely young lady. She had looked forward to many grown-up things she'd seen her sister doing. My mind flashed back to her arrival and the many pleasures she had brought to our family.

Fall of 1953 had been an exciting time for our family when the new baby's arrival date neared. My Mother visited, helping me harvest and process garden crops and to be there when the baby came.

The morning of October 2nd, my husband left for work and Mom and I prepared corn and cabbage salad to can. Carole eleven, Phil ten, and

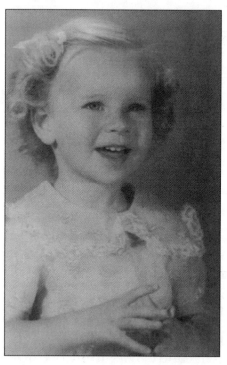

Susan, age 2 in 1955.

Tom five and a half, were getting ready for school when I realized the baby's arrival time had come.

I called them together and explained, "Our baby is coming today. Phil, you go tell the neighbors as we've planned, I'm having pain and must get to the hospital." Excitement grew but there was concern for me too. Carole said, "Please, Mama have them let us know about you and if we get our baby sister"

"We will dear, Daddy will call Gramma so you will know." I made preparations leaving

Mother in charge and to finish canning the big pan of corn and cabbage. My two neighbor friends took me to the hospital and notified my husband.

Pud did retail lumber delivery and by the time he reached the hospital he was father of another daughter. After seeing the baby, he lovingly touched me saying, "You've done it again, given me another beautiful baby." The baby was named Susan Elaine and in three days we went home. Excitement spilled over upon our arrival, everyone talking at once.

"Hurry in Mom, and get her unwrapped so we can see her."

"Let me look at her."

"Oh, Mom, can I hold her?"

Love and affection burst through the house while I carefully unwrapped Susan for all to see.

Each child was thrilled and wanted to hold her, Tom immediately wanting to take her to kindergarten for show and tell. Carole, due to crippling from polio, could not carry her, but Phil would take Baby Susan to her. Having been Carole's best buddy since they were small tots he sensed her wishes.

Our tiny tyke grew with more than her share of loving attention from her three siblings. Susan was important to them. They enjoyed watching her grow and loved teaching her new things.

I thought of how Susan could eat a bowl of chili and leave all the beans in the bottom of the bowl, cleaned off neatly because she didn't like them.

Susan at age 4.

Susan had played with her dolls and stuffed toys by placing them at her small table and chairs. She held Sunday school and many tea parties with the dolls carrying on grown up conversations. When the party was over she placed them in the doll buggy and pretended to take them home.

Susan loved listening to Tennessee Ernie Ford. She knew exactly when to turn the TV on for his program. When he signed off with his "Goodbye, all you little pea pickin' buddies"; she felt it especially for her and would kiss him on the screen. Our screen often needed the smears cleaned off. She knew when Red Skelton came on, too.

During Vacation Bible School in 1959, Susan was selected as a princess for the final program and received a pink crown to wear. Her brother Tom was chosen King for learning the books of the Bible and the most memory verses. His crown was gold.

When arriving home I said, "Put your crowns on and we'll take your pictures."

"I'm going to wear the gold crown." Susan said.

"No, it's Tom's because he earned it. You put your pretty pink one on."

Taking the gold crown and giving it to Tom and the pink one to Susan made her unhappy and needed more explaining. Susan is not smiling in our album picture of them in their crowns. This reminds me of another picture where her expression is similar; she and cousin Marty were playing with a tree frog when time for pictures arrived. She didn't get to hold the frog. This was

Tom and Susan with their crowns from Bible School.

a sharing lesson she had to learn. Most of the time she was a pleasant, loving child.

Susan, looking forward to school in the fall, awoke early one summer morning. She rushed barefoot in her nightie to the garden where I was working. "Mama, what if I don't know which desk is mine at school?"

"It will be ok, honey, the teacher will show you where to go."

Relieved, she immediately returned to her bed.

While traveling Susan said, "What will I wear my first day? Will I know many kids? I hope I like my teacher. Will I be able to read?" Her young mind was busy with thoughts and mysteries of school.

Carole, having improved from polio with surgery and therapy, took sewing in high school home economics class. With additional help from her paternal Grandmother, she became an excellent seamstress. Through the years she sewed many of Susan's clothes and lavished love on her by fixing her hair and tending her necessary needs.

One day after Carole had made Susan a new dress and fixed her up in it, I'd said to Pud, "Susan has truly been a gift from God for Carole."

"Yes," he replied, "she's been a blessing to Carole, and she's filled our home with a special love."

Phil and I had prayed Susan would be found alive. I sobbed over her not having the opportunity to experience her first day of school, to grow and enjoy a well rounded life. We now learned God's plan was for the happiness she brought to others in her short time on earth.

With Susan, all bodies of our loved ones had been found. I've always felt death must have been instant for them and pray they had no suffering. How thankful I am they could be given a Christian burial in our home town. Sadness gripped me with heart throbs for each of my lost loved ones. I had only Phil, and thoughts of our life without the others seemed impossible to comprehend. However, I knew I would do my best to raise Pud's son, now my only child, as he would have wished.

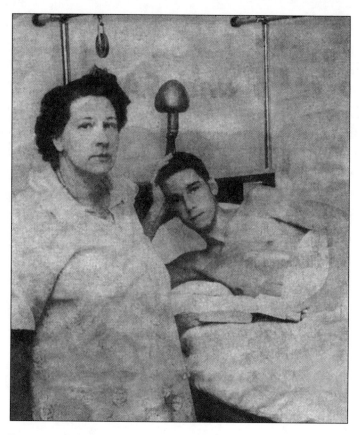

Irene stands beside her son's hospital bed as she prepares to leave the hospital. The Butte, Montana, newspaper praised them for their courage. (Reproduced from a Montana Standard *newspaper clipping.)*

Chapter 8

Family and Visitors

Our families experienced extreme frustration upon hearing news of the quake. After a multitude of anxious phone calls, my sisters located us through the Red Cross. The Red Cross had brought tooth brushes, robes, and other necessities to Phil and me at the hospital.

Seeing family when my sisters and their husbands (Ruth and Kermit Kiebert and Lois and Jim Burkhart) arrived made a slight bright spot in this sad time. We hugged and wept, sharing sorrow over our family loss. Lois said, "Irene, we know from our Christian rearing to put faith in the Lord. We don't expect to understand everything. Continue to keep your trust in Him."

With our loved ones' bodies found, my brothers-in-law identified them. My sisters and husbands spent a day with Phil and me before returning home. Ruth, worried about getting back to Mom, said, "We must get back to Mom and let her and Pud's folks know we've found you and you're with caring people."

I remember her telling me later, "Irene when I saw you, the hole through your lower lip had caused a swelling grapefruit size, and your hair looked like mud daubers attempted building a nest in it. We couldn't believe how your scraped and battered bodies had been thrown around. You were fortunate to have someone watching over you and be where you could receive such outstanding care."

With my lip swollen so big, I remember thinking, I'll never be able to wear lipstick again and look nice. The hole went clear through and not only looked like a grapefruit but felt like one. The nurses brushed my hair with dry shampoo after working many days to get all the moss and twigs out of it.

Finally one morning a nurse said, "I think we can give you a real shampoo today."

"Oh good," I said, "it will be great to have my hair clean."

Our next visitor, my brother-in-law Jack Bennett, hired someone to fly him to Ennis from our hometown of Coeur d'Alene. Jack took

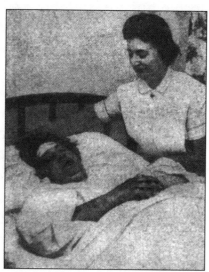

Nurse Mona Reed tends to Irene at the Ennis hospital. Notice her badly battered arm and swollen lip. (Reproduced from a Montana Standard *newspaper clipping.)*

over many responsibilities of our lives, handling our business affairs in Coeur d'Alene. The grandparents cared for our home place but their stress in coping with our loss caused Jack even more obligations.

Our pastor, Jack Hawthorne, of the Nazarene Church in Coeur d'Alene came with the mortician. Decisions for burial services troubled me but these two gentle men helped me through. Faith in God is for when one doesn't completely understand. I needed a touchable link to my Lord at this time and talking with my Pastor supplied this urgency.

Funerals were scheduled for August 26, 1959 and my sister-in-law, Beryl Ann Decker and her son Allan, came to comfort Phil and me. They shared our tears and gave us news of things at home with the grandparents and all. Pastor Hawthorne and Jack Bennett completed funeral arrangements and Jack's wife, Marian, picked clothes for the family's final rites.

My Mother (Myrtle Coulthard) soon came from Hope to be with us.

"Oh, Mom, how good to see you!" I cried upon her entering my room. She grasped me in her arms while we hugged and I sobbed. "I've needed you and your love."

"I was anxious to come but wanted to attend the funerals. I felt if your sisters came, then later I could stay with you and Phil for a little while. The train ride and bus connections were difficult but seeing you and Phil makes me feel better."

Mom visited back and forth from my room to

Phil's. We worried about him because he showed emotion but didn't cry. One day she came back to my room saying, "Phil thinks he has lost an ear."

"Oh Mom," I said, "Go right back and tell him he has both his ears. Tell him there's a bad cut behind one and it's draining but will be ok." Bandages encircled his head making it understandable he'd wondered.

After she told him, he sighed with relief, "Oh, thanks Gramma for telling me. I felt like maybe I only had one ear."

Even through my grief and shock I'd been thinking of our future. One day I asked, "Mom, what would you think if I went back to school? You know I always wanted to be a teacher, but couldn't attend college during the Depression. Since I'm living in a junior college town it's a good opportunity to take training. I've been out of school 21 years but I don't want just any job all my life. I'd enjoy working with children since I've lost my kids."

"I think it's a great idea. Perhaps you and Phil can go to school together," she agreed. This made my decision definite.

Chapter 9

Surgery

My thoughts flash back to Phil's surgery as I recall Dr. Losee saying, "I'm going to have to operate on Phil's leg before infection begins because the bone is working out through the flesh. I'll do my best but someone more powerful than me controls your lives."

This reminded me of Philippians 4:13, "I can do all things through Christ which strengtheneth me."

After healing and exercises I could go to Phil's room to spend time with him. Phil found it difficult to talk about family but still never cried.

We discussed surgery after Doc suggested a spinal. I hinted to Phil, "Spinal anesthesia's a bit scary to me because of paralysis incidents during World War II."

"Mom, I would like to have a spinal so I'll know what is going on."

I prayed for guidance and later went back to Phil saying, "I've signed the papers; you can have a spinal." He smiled.

The day of the surgery, they wheeled Phil by my room on the gurney, with him calling, "See you later, Mom."

Anxiety overwhelmed me during the operation. Time dragged and I prayed, "Let this surgery be successful and let feeling return with everything functioning properly."

At long last, on his way back to his room, Phil called. "Hi Mom, I heard the whole operation. I could hear them working on my bones. You'll have to see the piece of bone Dr. Losee took out. It's about two-and-a-half inches long and one inch wide with a jagged point."

I felt my prayers answered for Dr. Losee received superb strength to perform the operation. Still a sleepless night overpowered me because of concern about paralysis. However when morning arrived immense relief and comfort reinforced me when a nurse reported, "Phil's feeling has returned and his whole body is functioning well."

A new patient moved into my room; she strolled about but didn't speak. I'd be asleep and awaken from her patting my covers. Still not a word. Several days passed before I told Dr. Losee, "I can't cope with this senile woman who doesn't socialize. She does weird things like checking water pipes under the sink and looking under my bed. I'm becoming a nervous wreck."

Doc said, "I can't see any wrong in putting a mother and son in the same room. We're going to move you. Phil is alone in his room now."

"Oh, it will be good to be with him. Maybe we'll be able to talk of our lives in the future."

I was moved into Phil's room and enjoyed being with him.

After a few days I told Phil, "I'm considering going back to school. Gramma and I talked it over and she thought it a good idea. What would you think? Is your Mom too old for college? We're alone now and must prepare for our future. I've always wanted to be a teacher and feel a strong need to do this."

"Mom, I think it would be great! You can do it. We're in this together. I'll do all I can to make your life happy."

Now to continue recuperation from grief and injuries and to proceed with definite plans. Though we found this a hardship, at least I thought where I might begin to earn our support. I felt a deep love and responsibility for Phil. This brave sixteen-year-old kid had become adult almost overnight to stand by me. Without him life would be unbearable.

Being together we talked over many things.

He asked, "Will we stay at the home place, Mom?"

"Oh, yes, the place is ours, and we'll heal and then think of schooling. With a junior college in our home town, we'll start our education and make other decisions when time demands."

I cried over the other children not growing up and never being a Gramma for many children. Phil joked saying, "Mom, I'll get you a dozen grandkids like you thought you'd have." How great to laugh a bit.

We shared the feeling of being watched over the night of the quake and sensed we had been spared for a reason. Phil's attitude gave me hope, knowing we could handle our life together.

Again I prayed, "Thank you Lord for saving my son and giving him strength and courage to help me through this tragedy while we make our lives whole again."

Chapter 10

Progress in Healing

By mid September our healing made great headway. My scrapes, bruises, broken bone, and deep thigh wound were improving and chest muscles had mended through exercise. Doc said, "Irene, I think you're able to leave the hospital now."

"I'd like to, but I hate leaving Phil."

"We'll take the best care of him. You stay at your sister's like you mentioned and we'll keep you posted on his progress," he comforted, putting his arm around me.

We'd talked of my renting a motel in Ennis so I could be near Phil, but finances and my condition made it impossible. My sister, Lois, and her husband made arrangements to come for me.

When they came she said, "You can stay with us till Phil is released. We'll keep in touch with him by phone and letters."

"It's hard leaving him, but I know he's in good hands."

Doctor checked me thoroughly. "This thigh

wound is healing great." He pressed on my neck, which was still tender. "Perhaps I should put a neck brace on you."

"I don't need one," I told him, and he didn't insist.

He looked in my ears saying, "We'll flush these again to be sure they are clear." Thus he flushed more sandy silt out of my ears which he had done many times the past month.

Gathering my few belongings I bid Phil "Good-bye" hugging him closely saying, "Take care, honey, and get well so we can be together. I love you so much! You're all I have now." Emotions overwhelmed me.

This rapidly grown up kid replied, "I'll be ok and we'll soon be together. Don't worry."

Lois, Jim, and I left on the long hard ride to Hamilton, Montana. I thought several times my head would fall off because of weakness in my neck. Perhaps having a brace would have been best.

Traveling to Butte we stayed overnight at Jim's mother's home. Everyone's helpful ways contributed great support. By the time we reached their home in Hamilton, I felt weak and worn out.

Upon arriving, I saw my nephew Jon, fourteen, and niece Linda, twelve, for the first time since the tragedy. These kids showed a stunned sympathy. Their little dog, Bootsie, seemed to sense my sorrow too. Look," I said to Lois, "Bootsie seems to sympathize. Watch her snuggle close to me like she senses I need compassion."

Lois and I talked and cried for the loss of our loved ones and their not having a chance to live full lives. We found we could laugh at fun memories too. I told her, "I'm thankful for my good memories to hold forever in my heart."

Looking up the 121st Psalm, which I'd prayed the night of the quake, I said, "Our Bible calls this psalm a traveler's hymn of trust in Jehovah. Isn't that a coincidence? I've always loved Psalm 121."

This family treated me wonderfully, letting me rest as I needed and making me welcome in their home. They took me for drives and I enjoyed the beauty of the trees and mountains.

One evening Jon needed help with his math. "Maybe I can help, Jon, I think I still remember how to do algebra." I looked at his problems and managed to help him.

After a time when I could get around better Lois said, "Let's shop for more comfortable clothes for you."

She went to J C Penney's downtown and talked to the manager. "I have my sister with me who was in the quake. I wonder if you'd let me shop a bit and take articles to the car for her to decide which she wants. It is hard for her to walk."

"Of course you can," he answered. "Look all you want and pick out several things to give her a choice."

Lois picked short housecoats. She brought them to the car and I made my decisions on which I wanted. We went home with several loose comfortable dusters. I appreciated her sisterly love and the caring people who helped me during this healing process.

Recuperating with supportive sympathy of this family while remembering my good life with Pud and the children rendered healing therapy. We put our faith in the Lord. The Bible says, "To everything there is a season ... a time to weep and a time to laugh."

The 121st Psalm reads:

"I will lift up mine eyes unto the hills, from whence cometh my help. My help cometh from the Lord which made heaven and earth. He will not suffer thy foot to be moved: he that keepeth thee will not slumber. ... Behold, he that keepeth Israel shall neither slumber nor sleep. The LORD is thy keeper: the LORD is thy shade upon thy right hand ... The sun shall not smite thee by day, nor the moon by night. The LORD shall preserve thee from all evil: he shall preserve thy soul. The LORD shall preserve thy going out and thy coming in from this time forth, and even for evermore."

Chapter 11

Phil's Release and Home Again

As time drew near for Phil's release, we shopped again. He needed clothes to wear home. We knew he'd have to split the pant leg for his cast so didn't buy much. We'd get more later.

From Hamilton, we'd stayed in close touch with Phil and by early October he could be released. Lois and Jim took me to Ennis to pick him up. How wonderful to see him. "Oh! Mom, it's good to see you," he said as he hugged me.

I told him, "You're looking great and I'm anxious to get you out of here."

After more hugs and kisses, he said, "Last night the hospital staff held a neat party for me. Let me show you all the presents I received. Look at this autographed book, "The Rising Arrow" written by Hughie Call, a local Montana author. Isn't it a neat gift? I'm already reading it and will always keep it. I sure realize the importance of friends."

We enjoyed his excitement of showing his gifts and telling of the wonderful farewell they had given him. Dr. Losee and staff had done everything in their power to heal our bodies and our spirits. The whole town had showered us with mementos and visits to help us endure. Teachers had helped Phil keep up his schooling so he could finish his junior year.

We showed him clothes we'd brought. He said, "I'll like getting out of these hospital gowns and into people duds."

Doc examined Phil, making certain he was ready to leave. He cleaned behind his ear, removing more moss from the wound before dressing it. "This leg is doing great and other than being a bit short I think you'll be able to do most everything." He split the pant leg to fit over the big cast and Phil dressed to leave. We gathered his possessions together.

Doc examined me too saying, "Looks like we best flush these ears again." He washed more silt from them, saying, "You were fortunate to have heavy thick eardrums for trash scarred but didn't pierce them."

"I'm surprised anything's left in there now."

Our good-byes to these people and thanks for the super care at the hospital made us feel like leaving family. They all gave us hugs and bid us loving farewells.

We stayed overnight in Butte and then on to Hamilton. We remained with my sister's family for awhile. They then took us home to Coeur d'Alene.

HOME! It would never be the same again. I had difficulty entering the house. Lois sensed our feelings and left her children in the car until we'd been through our first sorrow.

Upon opening the back door I sighted Pud's red plaid chore jacket hanging where he'd left it. My thoughts racing back, I visioned him putting it on to tend the livestock. My heart throbbed knowing I'd never see him again. I knew I would wear this jacket for I clutched it and sensed his smell.

A few more steps into the kitchen and I looked towards the drawer where Susan kept her toys. My mind visualized her sitting beside the drawer deciding which toy to take out for play.

Going on into the other rooms, I glanced at Carole's salt and pepper shaker collection which began when she had polio. She displayed this growing collection with pride. On a shelf in the hall to the boy's room sat Tom's little miniature horse collection with some of his special rocks, another of his hobbies.

Other memories bounced off the walls and the furniture. I fell apart and cried, but Phil again shed no tears. Without delay he took me in his arms, and comforted me, holding me close as though I was the child. This made me sense this young man had taken on adult responsibilities and would be there for me. We had a hard task ahead but needed to settle in, bear these trying times, and move on with our lives.

Lois and Jim stayed a few days, then my sister

Ruth, and Mother came. Mother stayed with us while we recuperated. Dr. Losee kept in telephone contact with us requesting x-rays and checking on how we were doing. Our family doctor, Dr. H.H. Greenwood, took care of our immediate medical needs.

After a time I began having shooting sensations in my thigh. I went to my Doctor, "What are these strange shooting pains in my leg? They feel like I'm being poked with a cattle prod." (a battery powered device to make cattle move.)

He chuckled, "It's your nerve endings rerouting around scar tissue repairing your system. It may be uncomfortable for awhile."

All our friends and relatives came to keep us company and share our sorrow. Two girls out riding their horses came first to visit Phil. Many friends came and brought him up on the news of the neighborhood and school. He needed their companionship.

Our minister called and the pastor from my mother's church in Hope came, too. She told me later, "Reverend Meyer was amazed at your faith in God, Irene. He said you didn't need him like he thought you would. Your faith is stronger than mine."

"Mother, you instilled my faith in me! As a child you took us to Sunday school and church. We grew up in a faith atmosphere with our parents and grandparents," I answered. "I think of Dad driving miles to get us to Sunday School while on vacation."

After being home sometime and feeling better,

we decided we wanted to visit the cemetery where our loved ones had been buried. This was a crucial emotional experience. While there, Phil at last shed tears, "Oh Mom!" I enveloped him in my arms, hugging him and feeling it a great release for him to cry and let out his sorrow. This time I held up for him. We now cried together which helped both of us.

Soon November came and time for Phil's cast change. Brother-in-law Jack Bennett helped as he invariably did if needed. He drove Phil to Ennis for the change and a check-up. The trip went fine and a new cast made all ok for awhile. Dr. Losee told Phil, "I want you and Mom back for a check-up before Christmas. We'll put a walking cast on you then."

Phil said, "That's great news! It will be good to put this leg down."

Our healing both physically and emotionally was progressing.

"Survivors of Quake Return to Home" the headline stated. The paper wrote: "A heavy cast worn by 16-year-old Phillip Bennet and loss of about 17 pounds in weight are the only outward evidences of the serious injuries the boy and his mother, Mrs. P. R. Bennett suffered in the August 17 Montana earthquake and slide which claimed the lives of four other members of their family. The two are shown here at their Dalton Gardens home where neighbors and friends by the score are calling daily to wish them well." (Reproduced from a Coeur d'Alene Press newspaper clipping.)

Chapter 12

Our First Christmas Alone

With Christmas approaching, time for us to have examinations in Ennis filled our minds. Phil would get his walking cast. We made reservations on the fast train. However due to holiday schedules Spokane depot called and we had to take the slow train, commonly called the milk run. Leaving Spokane earlier than planned, we stopped at every little station. Phil said, "I guess this is a milk run as they only pick up milk cans at these stops." Clank! Clank! Then Chug! and on again to the next little whistle stop.

This being Phil's and my first long train ride I said, "I thought we'd be on the fast train and not have this stop and start, whistle and clank, but we'll manage."

At first we had room for Phil to put his big cast up on another seat. However as the train filled with college students returning home for the holidays, the conductor advised, "Let's move you folks to the smoking car where the boy can put his leg up and be more comfortable." The conductor helped us into the club car. We found it filled with old men, pipes hanging from their mouths or cigars in hand, the air filled with blue smoke. This is better? I wondered. Phil did have room to put his leg up even if breathing left much to be desired.

As dinner time neared I suggested, "Let's go to the dining car for dinner. We need a break from this smoke and since we only ate sandwiches for lunch we need a good meal."

"That sounds good to me, if I can manage to get there."

"We'll make it," I answered.

We started for the dining car, a real task for Phil on crutches moving down the aisles around feet and still keeping his balance. Our next trial, getting from one car to another, proved a bit hazardous but we engineered our way. Reaching the dining car a most polite black man seated us at a lovely table with a white linen tablecloth and napkins. Each place had beautiful silver service and sparkling glassware; a most elite surrounding. What a joy to be served a delicious meal in a pleasant atmosphere with NO SMOKE.

When we finished Phil said, "It would be nice to stay longer but I guess we best go back." So we retraced the previous difficult route to smoke and the old men.

The train pulled into Bozeman at midnight. We passengers disembarked staring down a long snowy cinder path to the depot. " Wow!" I said to Phil, "We must be at least a mile from the station. I can handle these two bags, if you can make it on crutches."

"Come on, Mom, we can make it. I just wish I could help with the suitcases."

Entering an unoccupied station, we found a phone and called a taxi which took us to a hotel. We managed to get a room together and requested an early wake up call. Arising from a few sleepless hours, we taxied back to the Bozeman depot where we'd arranged to be met on the fast train schedule.

Dr. Losee's nurse met us and took us to Ennis. Doc and his wife, Olive, had invited us to stay in their home when Phil had been there in November. We received wonderful hospitality, and their two young children welcomed us, too. Being Christmas time we enjoyed the beautiful decorations in their home.

One evening Olive said, "There's a Christmas service at our church tonight. Would you like to attend with us?"

"Yes," I answered. "We're missing programs and observances in our own church by being away."

We attended services in their small church which sat secluded on the corner of a snowy lawn. We sensed the reverence of the happenings in our lives and gave thanks for our care.

The following day Dr. Losee examined us both. He said, "Phil, we're going to take your cast off and leave you without it awhile. Olive and I are taking you and your Mother to dinner at a local restaurant. We want to treat you to a mouth-watering Montana steak dinner."

We went to the local cafe and had super rib steak dinners. After eating Phil said, "I'll be glad to get back into a cast; my leg feels like it's falling off."

Doc answered, "When we get the walking cast on you can begin to bear weight on it."

After leaving the restaurant, Doc and Phil went to the hospital for the new cast. When they returned to the house Phil said, "Gee, Mom it's good to put some weight on this leg and great to have support again."

Our exams over and all ok, we packed, and on December 22nd, my 40th birthday we left Ennis, boarding the fast train this time at Bozeman. My sister and husband met us in Missoula taking us to their home in Hamilton. Lois had a beautiful angel-food cake with a delicate vase of lovely flowers in the center for me. We celebrated by having cake and ice cream and remained in their home for the holiday.

Our first Christmas without our loved ones! Very difficult, but Lois and family did all they could to make it merry for us. Amidst all her preparations for Christmas I thought back to how Carole and Phil always helped clean house and crack nuts for baking and candy making. I visualized the gingerbread house which Carole and her Gramma Bennett made when she was nine. Each year she arranged it with our tiny porcelain manger scene beside it. I remembered each

Christmas eve reading the nativity story from the children's Bible storybook and how when the older children grew they read it to the younger ones. I thought of the scenes in the Christmas book Tom drew for me when in 3rd grade. I remembered him sneaking the wrapped gift into the house and hiding it. Then on Christmas morn he proudly presented the precious booklet. His drawings of the Holy night included Baby Jesus in the manger, Joseph, Mary, the shepherds and the wise men. It is priceless.

Other scenes flashed by me, one of Phil working hard repairing and repainting my old doll buggy for Susan's special gift; or when Carole sewed the bridal outfit for Susan's doll. I pictured Susan's excitement waiting for Santa and how the other children made it fun for her. I remembered the lovely gifts Pud always gave me and his wanting to be sure we had the best possible Christmas for our kids. All this flashed through my mind – priceless memories to hold forever.

Lois and Jim drove us around Hamilton to see the town's many pretty lights and decorations. While in Montana we enjoyed the beauty of snow capped peaks and the enhancement of sparkling frost crystals on every bush and tiny weed. What a beautiful winter wonderland! One morning I said, "Jim, I have to admit Montana does have magnificent beauty and a great amount of sun though temperatures are cold." He'd always kidded us how much better Montana weather and scenery were than Idaho.

They tried in every way to make our holiday

season homelike. We went shopping. I bought Phil a set of bongo drums for his enjoyment. He gave me a watch to replace the one I'd had on at quake time. We all had gift exchange and Lois prepared a delicious Christmas dinner. She served the traditional family meal of turkey, stuffing, potatoes and giblet gravy, candied sweet potatoes, our family's favorite shrimp aspic salad, cranberry-orange relish, and pies for dessert. Considering everything, we had a pleasant day.

We all went to my sister Ruth's home in Hope for New Year's. She fixed a luscious roast goose dinner with many of the family favorites and did her best to make us comfortable. Mother and we girls shared our loss and also pleasant memories. Ruth's little guy Marty, four, showed sympathy and expressed his sorrow by patting my knee and saying," Don't cry, Auntie, you'll be all right."

After enjoying our holidays with families as best we could, we went home. Phil's friends visited and took him sleigh riding on a sledge; a broad homemade platform with runners. This apparatus drawn behind a tractor whipped around corners to the delight of all. Sometimes Phil rolled off and into snow banks. The kids helped him back on and off they went. We'd wrapped his leg in plastic to keep the cast dry but he returned soaked and grateful he could experience fun times again.

People the United States over still sent us compassionate letters and donations to help us out. This made us realize how wonderful folks can be in times of need. I shed tears reading expressions of tender feelings and realizing how many generous people there are in this world. Through the years since our tragedy, I've tried to repay some of the thoughtfulness we received by sending donations to those whom I feel need assistance. I've sent to earthquake victims, people in war-torn countries like Rwanda and Zaire, and missionaries in Siberia plus individuals in times of disasters. We give toys and I make mittens for Toys for Tots. Returning kindness for kindness gives one a worthy feeling.

Chapter 13

Back to School

Phil entered school the end of January; a real struggle carrying books and handling crutches. His leg was healing as well as could be expected. It was a bit short, but with Dr. Losee's orthopedic expertise Phil became capable of doing most everything.

My Mother called one day saying, "A friend of mine here has a car he will sell you. Are you interested?"

"Yes," I replied. "We need a car since ours was destroyed. It will help not being dependent on someone else for everything. I could take Phil to school; riding buses is difficult for him. Later he can drive himself part time."

My brother-in-law checked out the car and thought it a good buy. The owner contacted me and delivered it to Coeur d'Alene. Having our own wheels helped us.

Years later Phil told me that after he was driving himself to school there were days when he couldn't take school. His thoughts were on the loss of the family. He just drove around. One wintry day he drove around Hayden Lake. He hit ice on a curve in the road and felt the car sliding toward a steep bank and possibly into the lake. He said, "I prayed. 'Don't let me die, I need to be here for my Mom.' I guess you know I had God as my passenger that day."

Phil, with his grief, still manipulated crutches and books and attended enough classes to complete his junior year.

In the spring my nephew, Kermit graduated from high school in Sandpoint, Idaho, and invited us to attend. I said to Phil, "This will be difficult for we'll think of Carole not graduating from Coeur d'Alene, but we'll go." We attended, but I cried, picturing Carole at her graduation.

At this time Ruth's fifteen year old daughter, Kay, wrote this poem in a creative writing class.

The Earthquake
Now when I think back to that day,
And all that God did take away,
It makes me sad, I want to cry,
For all of those who had to die.

The earthquake gripped the earth and shook,
Each closed his eyes, he could not look,
The fearful sound made people quiver,
The mountain fell into the river.

The eyes of God were open wide,
For He's our Father and our guide.
He's taken them for it was best,
I do not understand the rest.

Summer approached and I'd recuperated enough to begin plans for college in the fall. I sent for my high school transcripts and wished I'd been a better than just above average student. Gathering my courage I made an appointment to take entrance exams. Fright engulfed me but I knew what I wanted to do. The morning of entrance exams, my body filled with anxiety, I headed for the college. The vice president sensed my nervousness and said, "Just do the best you can, Mrs. Bennett, you'll be fine." Somehow I survived the strain and my results weren't bad.

Upon arriving home, I said to Phil, "Well, I made it that far. Orientation day will tell me more."

"You'll do ok, Mom."

In late summer Beta Sigma Phi sorority invited me to a tea. The college president and vice president attended, and President Kildow presented me with a grant from the sorority to help with my college expenses.

Opening day I attended orientation, took the English placement exam and arranged classes at North Idaho Junior College twenty-two years after finishing high school.

Reaching home I told Phil, "Guess what? Your Mom is not going to be placed in bonehead English class. I thought sure that's where I'd be."

"Great, Mom, I knew you'd do ok."

First day of classes seated me among the ranks with kids my daughter's age, actually many of Carole's classmates. I wondered if I could accomplish what I had in mind.

On this first day a girl next to me said, "Mrs. Bennett, I've attended school with Carole ever since junior high and when seated alphabetically you are in the exact seat where Carole would have been." These former classmates accepted me and Roberta became my lab partner in biology class.

My nephew, Kermit, came and lived with us to attend college and Phil went on to his senior year. Then began an experience trying at times, but I wouldn't trade those years for anything. Living with two young fellows helped keep my mind busy. They joked and teased, sometimes outvoting me but we got along great. Each did their share, all for one and one for all. Whoever got home first started dinner and things went fine.

I worked hard and at times felt the cogs in my brain had rusted beyond working again. My English class went ok but – biology! I felt I'd never learn it. Having attended school long ago when little science had been taught, I felt lost. I went to the professor and asked, "Would you please drop me from this course? I'm just not getting biology."

He said, "No way will I drop you, Mrs. Bennett. You are doing as well as some kids right out of high school."

"Well," I hesitated, "I guess I can continue." Thus I did stay with it and passed the course with above average grade. Later, when teaching, my valuable knowledge made me grateful the professor insisted I finish the course.

Grampa and Gramma Bennett became ill and moved from Coeur d'Alene to live with a daughter at Colburn, Idaho near Sandpoint. Gramma became extremely ill, and I'll always feel that the shock and death of the family was too great for her to bear. In late September we lost her.

Kermit, Phil, and I spent many weekends at my sister Ruth's and Mom's and had always visited the Bennett grandparents. Grampa always asked, "Well, how is school going?" We would give him the rundown on classes. He seemed pleased with my decision to attend college.

When holidays approached we spent them with family. The strong hurt of our loss caused me to be depressed, but with God's help and guidance I survived. Holidays have become easier through the years. Time heals some, though the scars remain forever.

Chapter 14

Return of Hope

New Year's Eve 1961, friends wanted me to go dancing with them. "No, I couldn't go," I said. "I'd feel like a fifth wheel."

My sis urged, "Irene, other singles will be attending. You need to get out with people. Jack Dunn and many of your former classmates will be there." After much persuasion I began tentative plans.

One weekend when at Ruth's, my niece Ruthann came into my room saying, "Auntie, Jack Dunn is having coffee with Dad. You better come out and see him." She knew Jack and I had kept company in high school, and she teased me a bit. "He doesn't have any hair and will look different than when you knew him." She'd worked for Jack in haying seasons and was his friend. Not having seen Jack since our late teens and now approaching our 40s, of course we had both changed.

I joined them in the kitchen for coffee and it

was nice seeing a friend from the past. This meeting broke the ice and I attended the dance.

I had a good time dancing and visiting with several old classmates and friends. I spent more time with Jack than the others and he asked, "May I take you home?" Little did I know how this would change my life.

Holidays over, Phil, Kermit and I went back to the routine of attending classes.

In February, we lost Grampa Bennett. I'm sure he died of a broken heart after losing Gramma on top of the loss of our family. Sadness enveloped me as I loved them both. They'd been good to me and we'd always been congenial. The Bennetts remain an important part of my life for I've stayed close to Pud's brother and sister and their families. In recent years I've researched Bennett genealogy so my son and his daughters would know more about their heritage.

Life moved ahead and feeling the necessity of continuing my education to maintain Phil's and my existence, I worked hard. One more year would complete my provisional teaching certificate with hope of finishing my degree later.

After meeting each other again, Jack and I corresponded and he visited me in Coeur d'Alene. We renewed our old friendship and caring for each other. How good to have someone my age to talk with and share my problems. Mother had spent time with us and I'd appreciated her, but this different caring filled a void.

Phil graduated with his class in 1961, and we invited Jack to attend graduation with family members. He and Phil seemed to get along well. Never having been married, Jack lived alone and ran a dairy farm. Strange I should find another dairy farmer.

In one of Jack's letters towards spring he said, "Sis is coming from California and will be in Lewiston visiting in-laws. Do you think we could arrange to go see her?"

I wrote back, "I'd love to see Maxine. We haven't seen each other since we worked in Spokane after high school. Do you think Phil and Kermit could milk your cows and care for the place? Phil has had experience with cows. If you do we'll make plans next weekend."

By this time Phil had become moderately active. Too much hiking in rough terrain caused strain but he had done some hunting in the hills around Hope. His limp was most noticeable when tired or in a hurry. Later he became able to skate, ski and participate in many activities.

The boys went to Jack's on the weekend to learn what would need to be done.

Jack said, "I'll mark the cows with red paint for you. Then you'll know which ones are dry and which are being milked. The cows know where to go when they enter the milking parlor."

Plans completed, we looked forward to the following weekend when Phil and Kermit would go to Hope on Friday.

They milked with Jack Friday night and Saturday morning to learn the milking routine, and all went well. Jack picked me up later Saturday morning and said, "It's strange being away. I haven't missed a milking in 13 years." Both our lives were beginning to change.

Maxine's relatives welcomed us in their home. She said to me, "I hope you and Jack will continue your friendship. I think you'd be good for him."I feel God had a plan for our lives. Jack had been alone a long time. He needed someone and I needed him.

We had a pleasant weekend, but during this time disaster prevailed in the Dunn barn. Not knowing the cows established milking order it seemed several cows wanted the same stanchion at the same time. One cow ate her grain and left the barn with the milking machine attached. Someone had forgotten to close the stanchion! Phil had a real chase for the bucket which dangled after her. Getting her back into the barn he finished milking her. It seemed they needed a number system along with the painting. So even though less milk appeared in the tank, they'd completed the milking job and Jack had gotten away to see his sister. Everyone enjoyed the weekend though milking had been a bit trying.

I began to sense God's mysterious ways for my heart beat not with sadness but with a renewed pulsation. Jack and I began renewing our love and speaking of marriage. I talked to my Mother who had lost my Dad at about the same age I lost Pud. She said, "Marry, Irene. Being alone is a miserably lonely life." Thus marriage became a serious subject.

We approached Phil with our plans and he said, "Great Mom! Dad wouldn't have wanted you to be alone."

I didn't attend summer school that year. Jack and I married on June 17th, my parent's 47th wedding anniversary date. I spent most of the summer with Jack finding there could still be happiness in my life though the hurt and loss of my family would always be with me. Having been happily married, and having the opportunity to marry again with my mother's and son's blessings, it felt right for me to begin again a happy life. The marvelous memories of Pud and my children will always be a precious part of my life. They cannot be taken away, and I've been fortunate to build more happiness to store in my heart forever.

Jack had known Pud and let me talk of the family and cry if I needed. Many times when I was overcome with sadness, he would take me in his arms saying, "Let it out, but you mustn't cry too long." This helped me cope. Nightmares still being a problem, Jack lovingly held me when I'd wake in tears. Love is so hard to define. Times when we find it most difficult to verbalize love may be when we feel and need it the most.

Chapter 15

More College Experience

When I returned to North Idaho Junior College in the fall, Phil went with me. We still had our home in Coeur d'Alene. Kermit came back to live with us and attend college, too. We continued spending most weekends in Hope with Jack finding life could be a happy time.

During Christmas vacation we put up our tree and Jack told us, "This is the first Christmas tree in this house since my Mother died when I was sixteen years old." We missed family members who weren't with us anymore but in spite of this, preparing a nice Christmas for Jack became our greatest joy. One of my best gifts was "Someone to love and someone to love me."

We spent part of our time with Mom and Ruth's family. Holidays over, we went back to school.

Towards spring I did my student teaching at second grade level in the Dalton Gardens School. Each of my three older children had spent a year in that room. Again this brought memories of those days.

One day the third grade teacher asked, "Would you like to spend one day in my room and hear the youngsters demonstrate their knowledge of phonics? These are the children with whom your Susan would have started school."

"Yes, I'd enjoy hearing them, and it will help me too." Walking into the room filled with little kids Susan had attended kindergarten with put a lump in my throat. As the children recited their phonics, I imagined Susan standing with pride to display her knowledge with these children. A difficult experience but giving me more determination to succeed with my teaching.

My student teaching under Donna Smith brought me joy and I knew I'd love helping other people's kids. I graduated in the spring with plans to attend summer school.

Phil and I busily prepared to complete our move to Hope. Jack and I chose the best of each other's furnishings to keep in our home. Driving back and forth I attended summer school. We discussed our life and I told Jack, "I want to teach at least a few years to use the knowledge I've gained."

He agreed, "If it's what you want."

With his blessing, I put an application in Bonner County School District for a job. My interview with the County Superintendent Jack Jones went well; in July I signed a contract for fifth and sixth grades at Clark Fork. Excited about teaching, I made many plans. At summer school I'd met Lois Westfall who taught in Clark Fork. Through our years of teaching together, I taught five of her children. We gained a lasting friendship.

After finishing summer school I spent time with Jack. Phil and his cousin Kermit visited the 1962 Seattle World's Fair. The following year they made a trip to Yellowstone Park. It seemed Phil felt a need to face the scene of our tragedy. Perhaps it was good for him, while I emotionally couldn't face it so soon.

During the rest of the summer, having rented my Coeur d'Alene place, we became permanently established in Hope. I called the Clark Fork principal and asked, "Could I get books and materials for planning my classes this fall?"

Mr. Anderson said, "I'll be going into the district office and will pick up material for you. I'll give you a call and you can come by."

"Thanks! I'll be anxious to hear from you."

My enthusiasm rose and excitement bubbled in me during preparation for my first year. I taught fifth and sixth grades for nine years and third and fourth grades for six years. I enjoyed the youngsters and loved reading good literature to them. We often laughed and cried together over stories. I'll never forget reading "Where the Red Fern Grows" by Wilson Rawls. It's a story of a boy and his dogs. The children loved it and begged each day for one more chapter saying, "We'll work extra hard and fast the rest of the day." One could have heard a pin drop while I read. Towards the end of the book when it became sad the boys and girls cried. We had to stop class while everyone took a break until emotions calmed.

Byron sobbing at his desk, got up and came to me saying, "Mrs. Dunn, What if that was my dog?" When his emotions settled down, he told me "This book will be the first one I'll buy for my children." Now you can get this story on video and hopefully many of them have seen it.

I remember Connie from the fourth grade class coming to my room one day after school. "Mrs. Dunn, I'd like to be in your room."

"Why?" I asked.

"My brother, Pat, says you're a fantastic reader. He says you choose the best books to read."

I enjoyed every child I taught and hope I did something for each of them which they'll remember. In ensuing years I've enjoyed high school reunions of former students including a twentieth of my first class of sixth graders and a tenth of my first fourth graders. Seeing these mature young people know where they are going in life delights me. I've attended showers, weddings, and receive Christmas cards, baby announcements and letters from former students. Being remembered feels great, knowing they too have pleasant memories of our times in class together.

During my second year in the classroom, I became acquainted with the Walkers as Harold became Clark Fork principal. Here again I gained true lasting friends. He and Harriet both gave good advice when I had any questions. Through the years I taught all four of their youngsters. I think of one thing Harold taught me, "Always keep a special two day plan on hand in case you need a substitute." I used his advice for many years. Giving the children a break from the usual and being back to present the everyday lesson the way I planned it to progress worked out well.

I continued summer college classes, sometimes finishing my school year at Clark Fork on Friday and being in Moscow at the University of Idaho for classes on Monday morning. Strenuous, but summer school and meeting new friends gave me encouragement. Evenings during the school year often consisted of extension courses and occasionally a correspondence course. This involved much hard work but I completed my degree in 1972.

Phil's second year of college away from Mom didn't go well. We'd had our rough times. I'd tried hard not to tie him to my apron strings, yet felt lonely when he went out. I'd never been in the house alone. After the quake I feared storms, and Phil came home knowing how alarmed I became. In my discipline I'd feel too harsh and wondered how his Dad would handle things. I'd ease up and find myself too lenient. Being a single parent was difficult, but we did survive. He'd grown up fast to be my strength; when I married Jack with someone else to care for me, he'd backtracked. He'd been too anxious to graduate in 1961 with the class he'd started with in first grade. Therefore he'd missed subjects which changed his courses at college and he felt confused about his future. Coming home, he worked in sawmills for a year and then took another semester of college.

Being unsettled about what they wanted, Phil and his friend John O'Donnell decided to take a trip and look the country over. With parents' approval, they left the summer of 1964 on a trip down the west coast and into Arizona where John's sister lived. They worked part time and stayed till spring. Phil didn't write as often as I wished and he sometimes received a letter saying only, "Hey, Your Mom would like to hear from you." Holidays and birthdays still saddened me, and Phil's and my first Christmas apart I found difficult. Jack and I sent him a popcorn popper among other gifts for he loved popcorn. Phil called, "Thanks for the popper, Mom. John's Mom sent him one too. Guess you both knew we liked it."

I must mention the gift Phil sent us. One day Jack brought a five pound box of chocolates from the Post Office. Laughing he said, "Phil sent us chocolates but forgot to mark them perishable. They are melted, squashed, and messy as possible. We'll see what's salvageable."

Looking it over I chuckled. "I'm sure he never sent a package before and had no idea how to prepare it for mailing." Phil had grown up in a home always having a big box of chocolates for Christmas. I guess he felt Jack and I should have them too. We thanked him but many years passed before he knew its condition on arrival.

Calling one evening from Phoenix, Phil said,

"Mom, John and I investigated a computer training school and for fun took a tour and a test. We both rated well. It's fascinating, the great expansion of the world through computer technology. Maybe this is what I want to do with my life."

"If you want that," I answered, "think seriously about it."

The boys came home and Phil reported, "John and I've decided we'd like to enroll in the fall for computer courses at the school where we took tests."

"Sounds ok if you think it's what you want."

Fall of 1966 found them off to Phoenix, Arizona to attend computer school. Feeling at last they'd found what they wanted in life, they'd left happy.

My Mother died in October and we grieved over the loss of someone so dear and important in our lives. We recalled memories of times from childhood to the present, knowing we'd miss her advice and sharing our pleasures with her. Though difficult, we endured another sadness for life goes on. Phil flew home for the grandsons served as pallbearers.

Returning to Phoenix, Phil and John attended school till early spring when they came home knowing they'd done well. Heading for Seattle to apply for work with Boeing, this happy pair soon returned with jobs. By April 6, 1967 they settled in an apartment there and went to work. Phil has been with Boeing ever since. He is now an administrative systems analyst with Boeing Computer Service, and with special training through the company has made good advances and a happy life.

This poem, "A Teacher's Prayer" by James J. Metcalf, I kept framed on my classroom wall. It expresses my feelings about teaching.

A Teacher's Prayer

"I want to teach my students
how to live this life on earth,
to face its struggles and its strife
and to improve their worth,
not just the lessons in the book
or how the river flows,
but how to choose the proper path
wherever it may go,
to understand eternal truth
and know the right from wrong
and gather all the beauty of a flower and a song,
for if I help the world to grow
in wisdom and in grace,
then I shall feel that I have won
and I have filled my place,
and so I ask your guidance, GOD,
that I may do my part
for character and confidence
and happiness of heart."

Chapter 16

Setback

Jack and I went on with our dairy farming and teaching. During the summer months we kept busy with haying, gardening, and upkeep on the place. I served the hay hands noon meals for I liked feeding hungry kids. One boy inquired after haying season was over, "Could I come back next year just for the meals? They've been good."

One hot summer, the kids requested, "Could we come early and work when it's cool?"

Jack told them, "It's ok with me. I just want the bales in the barn."

"I'll cook breakfast for you instead of dinner." I told them.

They came early and at 8 a.m. I served them pancakes.

While piling berry jam on a pancake, one boy remarked, "Boy, these homemade jams and jellies make these great!" They now finished by noon and had the hot afternoons for swimming.

Along with feeding the boys, canning, freezing garden and orchard produce kept me busy. I'd always loved canning for my family.

The summer of 1967 we took a boy, Bill Chatham, to live with us and to help during haying season. He'd been living with the Walkers at Clark Fork. Harold had come by and asked, "Could Bill stay with you while we're on vacation?"

"Yes," Jack replied, "I can use him in the hayfield."

He and Jack got along well and towards school time Bill approached Jack, asking, "Would it be possible for me to stay with you folks during the school year?"

"Yes, as long as you help with chores around the place."

Bill saw things which needed to be done and helped Jack a great deal. They worked well together and Bill gained knowledge from working with and for Jack. He lived with us through his graduation in 1969 and we learned to love him like our own. Prior to this time we'd looked into adoption but with my teaching it hadn't worked out. We'd even tried to take in a foster child. Someone above watched over us and things worked out, for with Bill both parties profited equally. Bill left for California in early fall of '69 to join the Navy.

On the 16th of September, Jack fell from the hayloft onto a concrete floor in the feeding shed. He didn't come to dinner and I called but no answer. Worried something might be wrong, I went to the barn still calling.

Conscious, he answered me, "I fell, I can't get up. I think I've had a heart attack and I'm bleeding from my ear."

Terrified I didn't go clear to him feeling I must summon help. Rushing to the phone I controlled my emotions and called the ambulance, my sis Ruth, and the Doctor. By the time I got back to Jack, my sis and nephew Kermit had arrived. Kermit said, "Don't come in, Auntie!" I didn't, feeling he thought it best I shouldn't.

While waiting for the ambulance I prayed, "Dear GOD, let my darling live. I'm not sure I could survive losing him."

Ruth took me to the hospital, following the ambulance. They didn't let me see Jack for some time. Finally Dr. Munson came and said, "We think he'll make it. We've cut these smelly barn clothes off him and he is a bruised and broken man. We don't think it was a heart attack."

The Doctor gave me the sack of dirty clothes. Why?? I'm not sure, they were garbage. Knowing Jack had cleaned the loafing shed a few days before made me sense his injuries wouldn't have been as bad with a thicker layer of cow manure on the floor.

Ruth stayed with me all night. Our heartfelt prayers continued. I spent a thirty-six hour vigil with Jack before I felt I could leave him. He cracked his skull in three places, had rib injuries, some broken and others torn from the sternum. His neck and shoulder were damaged, his wrist broken and paralysis encompassed one full side. I wanted to hold this black and blue darling close to me, but felt I didn't dare touch him. I just thanked the Lord; he'd heard my prayers.

I'd called Phil, and he came on the first flight available. He told his friend as he left Seattle, "I don't know what I'll do with my Mom if she loses another loved one."

When arriving at the hospital he found me crying. He looked panic stricken as he grasped me in his arms. I quickly said, "Jack is going to live. These are happy tears."

"Oh Mom, I'm so glad. I'll stay and do chores and bring you back and forth to the hospital."

My sister Ruth had been my great stabilizer. Through all my problems she helped any way she could, as she'd done my entire life. She'd taken me back and forth to the hospital till Phil came. How true, "a sister is a forever friend." Both my sisters have been faithful in time of need; when tragedy struck in 1959 and during Jack's accident and recuperation.

I worried about Phil's job as he stayed with us so long. Tom Brown, Phil's boss from Boeing called, "Mrs. Dunn, we are wondering how Mr. Dunn is doing. Boeing would like to offer blood or help in any way we can."

"Thank you. Jack is doing as well as can be expected. He'll have a long recuperation but is improving. I'm concerned for Phil's job with his being away so long."

"Don't worry, Mrs. Dunn, keep him as long as you need him. He'll have a job when he gets back."

What a relief to know that!

After being in the hospital for sixteen days, Jack's paralysis gradually left his side. When we brought him home his left arm and hand were regaining strength. I'd taken leave from teaching to care for him.

Having written Bill in California about Jack's accident, he soon came. Upon arrival he told us, "I'll stay, take over chores, and Phil can go back to his job in Seattle." We appreciated Bill for he took over efficiently knowing Jack's routine well. Phil returned to his job, and Bill stayed with us till late spring when Jack sold the dairy cattle knowing he'd never be able to milk cows again.

Jack required lots of therapy and nerve shock treatments in Spokane, Washington, the closest place for him to see a neurologist. Again Ruth and family helped out.

The Doctor gave us a small shock machine to use on his arm at home. I measured salt in my hand to put in the water and proceeded to prepare for treatment. Watching, Jack said, "The Doctor said use a teaspoon of salt."

"I did."

"You just put it in your hand."

"Yes, but it was a teaspoon."

"Are you sure?"

"I'll show you." I started over, getting a spoon and salt. I measured in my hand and put it in the teaspoon. A perfect measure. After this he never again questioned my measurement of salt for his therapy. It gave me a good feeling for this told me he was getting well and back in control of his life.

Jack soon could do things but will always

have problems from his accident. People say he looks like he always did. They have forgotten; I haven't. One eye is affected, and when he is tired his face draws down and his speech slurs. He often needs therapy for his injured shoulder and neck. But the amazing, important thing is he's here and we are thankful to God!

Chapter 17

Jack and I

I wrote this story in 1986 about Jack and me. I feel it shows God's plan for our lives and think it fits in this story.

Our Fairy Tale Love Story

Our Hope School was having the first party of the year, 1937. As I entered I was attracted to a new young man. We became acquainted and at the end of the evening, Jack asked to escort me home. Soon we began going together to all the school festivities and the Saturday night Community dances. At graduation time, spring of 1938, we exchanged pictures. Soon we became too serious for young people, and on a friendly basis went our separate ways. For some unknown reason we did not give back our pictures. Later events prove we lack complete control of our lives.

Going off to college, joining the Navy, and being involved in World War II, Jack's life was busy. With the war over, he came home to care for his Dad until his death. Jack then ran a dairy farm alone at his home place.

After Jack and I parted, I dated a friend I had gone with at times and we fell in love and married. We lived on a dairy farm and reared our family. With Pud and our four children, I was very happy until tragedy struck in 1959. While on vacation, I lost my husband and three of our children, in the 1959 Montana-Yellowstone Park earthquake. Carole was seventeen, Tom eleven, and Susan almost six. I loved my husband very much and with this tragedy felt my life's happiness ended. Nonetheless, from necessity and with the grace of God, my surviving sixteen year old son and I together salvaged our lives.

I went back to college, earned my teaching degree, later teaching for 15 years enjoying other people's children. During these years while visiting family at Hope, I met Jack again at social gatherings. We were still attracted to each other and our past teenage romance blossomed into real adult love. We began dating and married with the approval of my son, Phil.

Jack and my son share a GREAT friendship. Phil married and he and Robin have given us three beautiful granddaughters. Jack is a WONDERFUL Grampa to "our" grandchildren. We are a family again, and I have happiness and a truly loving marriage. Jack's and my senior pictures, which we kept all these years are together in a double frame on our dresser.

This fairy tale love story is definite proof someone more powerful than ourselves has complete control of our lives.

Jack and Irene Dunn in 1995.

Chapter 18

A Surprise Spring Break

Jack continued to make improvement during the winter, and I returned to my teaching second semester. When spring break approached, joking, I asked, "What are we going to do during spring break?"

"Maybe we'll fly to Seattle and visit Phil." I thought he can't be serious. Shocked I said, "Are you able to make a trip? Besides I never thought I'd fly." We talked it over and began making serious plans. Bill would do our chores and care for the place.

When I called Phil to say we might come over he answered, "Great Mom! Are you sure Jack can stand the trip?"

"He feels he can, and it will be nice to get away from the work he sees needing to be done."

"Oh, I'll show you all around Seattle! We'll tour Seattle Center. I want to take you to Ivar's for seafood dinner. I know a Chinese restaurant you'd like. It will be fun showing you the sights."

After making arrangements for both at home and with Phil we made reservations to fly over during spring break. When we boarded the turbo-jet I had butterflies in my tummy. We sat right over the wings. Looking out the window after take-off and seeing the wings move, I asked, "Jack, do you think we'll get where we want to go? Look at the wings flap."

Laughing, he said, "We'll make it. They're not flying this plane if it's not safe." Of course we made it, and I later learned to love flying.

Phil met us and we went to his and John's apartment. We received a great welcome. Their apartment shined. The bed had bright flowered sheets and pillowcases which they'd purchased especially for the occasion.

For the next few days Phil showed us the sights; Seattle Center, the Space Needle, Woodland Park Zoo, and we rode the monorail. Jack stood all the festivities well. At the zoo Phil suggested, "Why don't you rest on the benches and watch the animals while I get us a cool drink?" Other times during our tours he'd say, "Let's stop and have a cup of coffee." He showed great concern that Jack not overdo.

One morning Phil said, "Today we're going on the ferry to Bremerton. When we return we'll have dinner at Ivar's down on the waterfront."

We had a beautiful trip over the water. Returning to Seattle, we went to Ivar's interesting seaside cafe where we all enjoyed a delicious seafood treat.

We visited other choice haunts of Phil's, eating

at his favorite Chinese restaurant and having lunch at select little cafes.

One morning he said, "I want to take you to the Pike Street Market. It's filled with fresh foods like in your garden. John and I get our farm fresh eggs there."

Venturing on our way he turned at the next corner, and I yelled, "Phil, you are going the wrong way on this one way street!"

"It's ok Mom, I'm only going one way."

We chuckled for we knew this error wasn't a habit. Fortunately there weren't any cars and it was only one block.

Entering, Phil said, "Isn't it great to see all this fresh produce available for city people to buy? Let's walk through and go into the seafood department, too. Come this way and we'll look at the ocean fish. I want you to see oysters, crab, lobsters and other fish fresh from the ocean which are for sale."

On our way back to the car, we admired the numerous crafts people had on display. Phil seemed amazed at all the merchandise available there.

Soon vacation time was over and we returned home, back to our routine of chores and school. Bill had taken excellent care of the place.

Our time with Phil had been a real treat, available to us only through Bill's help. We now stored these memories for later recall.

The cattle sold in May for Jack would not be able to dairy anymore. Bill left and joined the Navy. After completing his basic training, he came home for a visit and then was off to Vietnam. We corresponded and I prayed for his safety. Bill did return home safely for which we were thankful.

Chapter 19

Meeting a New Person

Often when Phil visited I hinted to him, "Perhaps you should find a nice girl."

He always answered, "I'm lookin', Mom."

In the summer of 1970, his friend John married in Sandpoint with Phil as best man. John said to me, "I think Phil has found someone he cares about. Maybe another wedding is in the offing."Late summer a call came from Phil, "I'd like to bring a friend over for the weekend. Would you please fix both bedrooms, Mom? I'm bringing a girl."

Excitement filled me as he sounded happy. He brought Robin Koskela, and we enjoyed meeting her. Phil loved showing off this attractive young lady though she seemed shy about meeting his folks. While we chatted and became acquainted, I served her coffee and goodies. Years later she told me, "I didn't like coffee but took it to be polite. I thought you'd never quit pouring."

In time we sensed a serious relationship

developing with these two. They soon made tentative plans for an April wedding. However at Thanksgiving we received this call, "Mom, we're married. This saves us paying rent on two apartments."

"I'm happy for you. Where were you married?"

"In a Methodist Church, Mom. John and Robin's friend stood up with us."

He knew I would like them having been married in a church.

With Christmas approaching Phil called, "We're coming to spend the holiday with you."

"Oh! That's great! What would you like me to fix for dinner."

"Tradition, Mom, tradition! What else? Be sure there's cranberry orange relish, shrimp aspic salad and pies." This season had previously been hard but now with an added member we were becoming a family again.

The young couple came and we had a wonderful Christmas; they brought gifts galore. At the end of this fabulous day, Jack said to me. "Sometimes I feel like Phil belongs to me. He's concerned about our well being and contented with our life. I'm happy we get along so well."

I couldn't have had a more precious gift. These two had become such good friends and the happiness of the four of us sharing gifts and a traditional meal had made a great holiday.

When spring break arrived, we visited Phil and Robin. She had their apartment fixed in tasty decor and it was an exciting experience being entertained in the home of my son and his wife.

We enjoyed their fixing special meals and taking us interesting places even though we soon had to return to the farm and school.

Robin worked for Boeing, too. After a year of working different shifts and not seeing a lot of each other she decided to quit work and be a homemaker. They visited us when they could, and we went there during school breaks. It made us proud to see their accomplishments. With Robin at home now, I said to Jack, "I wonder if I might become a Grandmother. Wouldn't that be a thrill?"

After living in apartments they'd begun to think of owning a home and proceeded to look. Phil called, "Mom, you know we've been looking for a place. We think we've found a nice home on a culdesac in Kent, Washington and I think we'll buy. When we get moved in we'll want you to visit."

We were in touch as they finalized the purchase and after they moved in Phil called, "Mom, I think you'll like our place. We want you to come soon. Robin has it decorated nice with her embroidered panels you saw her working on when you were here."

We made a trip over as soon as arrangements could be made. What fun seeing them have a home of their own and show pride in their acquisition. We enjoyed being in touch and knowing about their life. Then early in 1973 a call came saying, "Mom, you're going to be Gramma."

"Oh, great! I'll love having a grandbaby.

When is this to be? Is Robin feeling ok?"

"She's fine and it will be early November. Maybe even on Grampa's birthday. Will Jack like being a Grampa?

"I'm sure he will, he's adjusted to you really well."

Phil chuckled, "I know, we get along great."

Just then Jack came in the house and I called to him. "Guess what? We're going to be grandparents. How's that, you being a Grampa?"

He laughed, "Well, it isn't every one who can be a Grampa without being a Daddy first. I'll like it, I love little kids."

I said to Phil, "He'll be happy to be Grampa."

"That makes my day." Phil answered,"I think he'll be a great one. We'll keep you informed how things are going."

Early summer we received an invitation. "We want you to come over and take a trip with us by ferry up through the San Juan Islands to Victoria and Vancouver, B C. Think about it and make plans."

In August when hay and fruit crops were in, we went to Phil's. They drove to Port Angeles where we boarded the ferry. After parking the car, we went to the viewing area where we could enjoy the ride and the scenery. The ferry stopped briefly at Orcas Island where many bicyclists disembarked to tour the island. Reaching Victoria, after a beautiful ride, we explored the waterfront. We visited the Parliament buildings and the Empress Hotel, shopped Hudson Bay stores and surveyed other interesting sights. We toured

Craigdarroch castle built by a wealthy Scotsman for his bride. Coal Baron Robert Dunsmuir built his castle with no expense spared. Having become a museum, it had many of its original paintings and furnishings. There's a huge ball-room on the third floor and on up narrow stairs one reaches the turret with windows all around and benches beneath. We were told the bride wrote letters home to Scotland from the turret where she could view the ocean.

We toured Buchardt Gardens enjoying the Rose Garden, Sunken Garden, Italian Garden, the Japanese Garden plus many beautiful fountains and ponds. Seeing one spectacular sight after another we oohed and aahed having a great time. Robin's pregnancy kept her from enjoying it to the fullest. Strolling and admiring the many gorgeous blooms, I would say, "We've lost Robin."

Phil would look, "She can't be far."

She wasn't really lost, we'd soon find her cooling off her puffy feet in a little pool of water.

"My feet ached," she'd say, "and all this water tempted me."

Off we'd wander only to lose sight of her again. She used the ponds several times to cool her swollen feet.

We visited Canada's largest oceanarium seeing the killer whales perform many antics along with frisky little harbor seals and sea lions.

From here we went by ferry again over to Vancouver, B.C. where we stayed in a high-rise apartment building. We enjoyed the totem poles carved by Indians of the Northwest and toured

Stanley Park seeing lots of marine life, fancy Eskimo carvings and numerous other sights.

We shopped the street sales and purchased a few items for the coming baby. That evening we ate in a fancy restaurant and Robin had flaming steak.

There was much more to see both in Victoria and Vancouver but with time limited we did the best we could. We returned to Seattle by ferry. Jack and I returned to Hope with many pleasant memories; and Phil and Robin went back to work.

Chapter 20

Becoming Grandparents

School started and of course I had to brag about the coming event of being a Grandmother. On November 12, 1973 our granddaughter, Mary Riann, arrived. Proudly I wore a sign saying, "I'm a Gramma." My friend, Harriet Walker, put a sign on the bulletin board announcing our grandbaby to the staff. Being anxious to see the baby we flew over to Phil's during Thanksgiving break. Phil met us and when arriving at the house I rushed in. "What a beautiful baby with peaches and cream complexion!" I exclaimed. "The Lord has given me so much after I'd thought my life over at quake time. I know now HE has a plan for each of us." It brought to mind Proverbs 3:6 "in all thy ways acknowledge Him and He shall direct thy paths."

During the next months we talked by phone, enjoying news of Phil and his family. We loved receiving pictures of the baby and seeing her growth. I remember the thrill as time progressed when Riann began to know us, and later on the phone would recognize my voice. Pride overtook us when she learned the alphabet and to count, and could sing and dance.

Sometimes they came to Hope and we visited them during spring vacation, and in August after harvest.

Time moved along and we spent it with this new family whenever possible. Another grandbaby was on the way and on August 6, 1975 we received a call, "Mom, you have another beautiful granddaughter."

"What are you naming her?

"Amy Irene. Mary Riann was named for Robin's Mother so this little gal has your name."

"She arrived on your Grandfather Bennett's birthday. Did you realize that?"

"No," Phil answered, "I didn't remember his birthday."

After harvest we could get away, and we spent a few days admiring these charming grandchildren. Amy grew rapidly and had a great love for Grampa Jack causing me to feel a bit jealous. He's made the girls a most spectacular grandfather.

I'll never forget when Riann called saying, "Gramma, I'm getting so big my legs come all the way up to my panties." What joy we shared talking to them and receiving pictures.

On one visit when Riann was four and a half she asked her Daddy, "Why do you call Grampa Jack and Gramma Mom?" Phil took her for a walk and explained about the quake and loss of his Dad and siblings. He said, "Jack's my step-dad."

She spoke up, "Then why don't you call him step-daddy?"

That summer Riann and Amy came to visit a week. Amy's first night without Mommy made bedtime difficult. But with comforting hugs she settled in ok. Riann wanted to know more about Daddy's brother, sisters, and his Daddy. We went through pictures together. She would hold them and look and look. She noticed right away Carole wore a brace. "Gramma, what's wrong with Carole's leg?"

I explained, "Carole had polio and was very sick when she was ten. It made her leg weak and she had to wear a brace to help her walk. After operations and lots of exercises she got better."

For such a young girl Riann's curiosity and questions amazed me. Amy looked at pictures but it was all a bit beyond her yet.

During the girls' visit on the farm we did many things together. They trailed Grampa wherever he went and watched what he did. They loved riding in the trailer behind the tractor. I read them stories, played records, and baked cookies with their help. One day while making peanut butter cookies Amy said, "How is my Daddy going to get any of these cookies?"

I fixed a container and said, "We'll freeze some for when Daddy and Mama come for you girls. Here, Amy, help me put some in here."

When the folks arrived Amy said, "Daddy, we have some cookies for you in the freezer. Let's get them, Gramma." Her eyes glowed as she said, "Riann and I put them on the pan for Gramma."

Years continued and we cherished our times together. Then Jack began having health problems and required surgeries. Due to these circumstances I took leave of absence from teaching in the spring of 1977 to stay home with him. Experience told me one never knows what's in store in our lives, and we needed time together. I enjoyed caring for and being with him, plus having time to read and do my crafts. He had a rough time for awhile but we enjoyed each other, and I decided not to go back to teaching full time. Jack's health became better and I did substitute work in classrooms where I knew the teachers' ways and enjoyed being back to teaching some. When I quit substituting I did volunteer work and some tutoring for awhile.

In the spring of 1978 I flew over to Seattle and took care of Riann and Amy while Robin was having a new baby. What good little girls – no problems at all. Phil called me at the house the morning of April 7 the day before his thirty-fifth birthday and said, "Another girl, Mom."

"Great, we love little girls."

"We're naming her, Lindsay Caitlan. Mom, your Dad had three girls, I guess it's ok for me. I'll settle for them because I think four women are all I can handle."

We laughed. "I thought after the quake you said you'd get me a dozen grandchildren. But it's ok. I'll settle for three lovely little girls."

Time changes things. We all of course, had

thought "boy" with this last baby coming, wanting to carry on the Bennett name. However, far more important are healthy babies, and we're happy with our three girls.

In the evening we visited Lindsay and Mom at the hospital. While viewing another beautiful baby, happiness surrounded us all. We had become a complete family again through God's tapestry of weaving throbbing heartbeats and heartaches into health and happiness.

Irene Dunn surrounded by family in 1997 portrait. Clockwise from the left: Lindsay, Amy, Riann, Robin, Jack, Irene and Phil.

Chapter 21

Complete Happiness

T hrough the years the girls grew and enjoyed visits to our farm. Since being home for Thanksgiving seemed more important for Phil than Christmas, they most always came then. We often had our gift exchange then, too. One year the little girls decided we should have a tree. Riann asked, "Gramma, can we decorate this tall plant to put our gifts around?"

"Yes, I'll find you some colored paper and you can make chains and other decorations." This started a tradition. Each year after this they made home-made decorations.

Grampa would say, "Come girls and we'll get a little tree for you to decorate." Going for the tree became an important part of Thanksgiving weekend. Now we had Thanksgiving on Thursday, went for the tree and decorated on Friday, opening Christmas gifts on Saturday. It worked out well. We never knew what the weather would be at Christmas and didn't want them traveling Snoqualmie Pass with these little ones.

I recall one year when four year old Lindsay had decided she didn't like her name and wanted to be called Charlie. Upon hearing her dragging a chair in the kitchen I went to her. "What are you doing, Lindsay?"

"My name's Charlie!" she said standing on the chair by the window. "Gramma, come look at the cows. This is how they wag their tails." I looked and she was wiggling her little behind.

The girls grew and we valued our times with this family. When they became older we began to exchange packages to be opened Christmas morning. Christmas day the phone rings with words of "Merry Christmas" and thanks going both ways over the lines. Through these years the girls have become young ladies. The older girls work and take college classes. Lindsay is a senior in high school and for a school project spends part of each Sunday rocking babies in a care home for addicted little ones.

We greatly enjoy each person in this wonderful family and share time together whenever possible. It is splendid being a family again. I quote William Barclay from one of Pastor David Parker's sermons cited in Philip Yancey's book "Disappointment With God" Chapter 21, Page 157. "Endurance is not just the ability to bear a hard thing, but to turn it into glory." This most fitting statement describes my finding a new life with God's help.

Epilogue

Having lost my family in the Montana-Yellowstone earthquake in 1959, I found a need to return to the scene after 36 years. With encouragement from my surviving son Phil, I became determined to prepare myself for the emotional experience of visiting the earthquake area. Phil and his wife, Robin, took my husband, Jack, and me to the area. A trying ordeal, but through prayer I'd strengthened myself for the visit.

Entering Ennis, we passed the Madison Valley Hospital where my surviving son and I had received care after rescue. This caused tears and a lump in my throat. Our Lord had watched over us as Dr. Losee had just returned from Orthopedic School, and Phil needed his expertise. Driving through town, we reminisced about a steak dinner we had shared with the Losees when there for re-examination and a walking cast for Phil at Christmas time that year. After renting motel rooms and contacting the Losees, Doc and his nurse wife, Olive, came and spent a pleasant evening with us. We became reacquainted, shared the experiences of past years and also laughed. Doc remarked, "One of the most important things in life is a sense of humor."

"I could never have faced life after my loss without it," I commented.

The following morning after breakfast in

Phil and Irene stand below the plaque erected near the landslide in memory of the earthquake victims.

Ennis we proceeded to the earthquake area. Intense emotion overwhelmed me upon approaching the site, but I swallowed the lump, shed some tears, gathered myself together and entered the interpretive center.

Arriving there moments before the video presentation, we sat down and did well until they spoke of the Purley Bennett family and quoted me. Jack reached for my hand and we all clutched hands, shed tears and listened. Fortunately I didn't fall apart as I'd feared. We toured the center and read papers about our family and comments by me. Rampant emotions enveloped me, but I managed to hold on.

At an opportune moment I approached the supervisor, Joanne Girvin, at the center and told her who I was.

She said, "You know Mrs. Bennett?"

I answered, "I am or was Mrs. Bennett."

"You're Irene Bennett Dunn. Your friend was

here last year and told me she knew you. She said you're writing a book. Are you on the tour bus?"

"No," I replied.

"When the tour bus leaves I want to talk to you."

This viewpoint above the memorial plaque shows the area of the landslide.

I told her we were going up to the memorial monument and would be back.

We hiked up to the monument where the names of those lost in the slide included our family members. We then went up to a higher viewpoint where Phil and I tried to orient ourselves by looking over the place where we'd been rescued. Only the mountain with the ridge from where we'd seen the dirt rolling from a fault line seemed natural. Of course a tremendous amount of dirt had been moved by the quake and then again by dozers to rebuild the area and its roads.

While there the supervisor came and we had a pleasant visit. She said, "You are the second and third survivors I've met in my five years here."

We had a good discussion with her of our experiences and also of the video presentation. I expressed that some of it bothered me as it was untrue. She asked us to keep in touch, saying she would like to have my book there at the center when finished.

Feeling this had been a successful trip brought me pride and confidence that I'd attained my goal and could now finish my book. While honoring my lost loved ones by visiting the site, I appreciated Jack, Phil, Robin and the girls, the loved ones who've brought happiness to my present life. We know God works in mysterious ways and time has helped us realize His plan. It is said He often breaks our hearts so He can beautify our lives.